*Beyond Chaotic Eating*

After working as a research assistant in the psychiatric department of a Zulu hospital, Helena Wilkinson trained ... counselling. For four years she was the Editor of *Carer* ... *Counsellor*. She is the author of six books and is a ... member of the Society of Authors and the Society of ... Women Writers and Journalists. Helena is the founder and ... director of Kainos Trust for eating disorders, a registered charity helping people suffering from anorexia, bulimia ... compulsive eating. She has lectured internationally ... eating disorders.

# BEYOND CHAOTIC EATING

*A way out of anorexia, bulimia
and compulsive eating*

## HELENA WILKINSON

RoperPenberthy Publishing Ltd
Horsham, England

Published by RoperPenberthy Publishing Ltd
PO Box 545, Horsham, England RH12 4QW

First published in Great Britain in 1993
by Marshall Pickering
Updated version published by
RoperPenberthy Publishing Ltd 2001

**ISBN** 1 903905 11 7

Cover design by Angie Moyler

Typeset by Avocet Typeset, Brill, Aylesbury, Bucks
Printed in the United Kingdom by Cox & Wyman Ltd,
Reading, Berkshire

*To all those who long for freedom.*

Although anorexia nervosa and bulimia nervosa are the medically correct names, for convenience the shortened versions of anorexia and bulimia will be used throughout the book.

Eating disorders affect both men and women, however, the feminine is used for simplification.

To protect people's identities all names of sufferers used in this book have been changed, except where quoted from previously published material.

# CONTENTS

# HOPE IN THE DARKNESS

Autumn in Britain is a time when the country is bursting with golden colours. As the leaves tumble to the ground some people can see only the bleakness of winter ahead. Yet out of winter, where everything is naked and exposed, grows spring, with all its vitality. It was in the autumn that I was asked to write a book on eating disorders. In the same month I attended the funeral of a seventeen-year-old anorexic girl, Pippa. She did not want to die; only to be thin.

Some of the words which Pippa wrote in her diary before she became anorexic speak of the terrible ache inside. They show the desperate feelings which exist before the illness, and the longing for someone to understand and reach out:

> "My life is going too fast. I can see it in front of my eyes. I never used to be able to. I don't understand it any more. 'Soon I will be back at school', I said before Christmas, 'and here I am now two days before school and so much work to do. I want to be thin. I know everyone says that. But I do, I really do. I hate myself. I am not pretty. I am no good at school, sports or relationships. What am I good at? I don't know! I get so depressed when I sit and think about these things. No one wants me. I saw it yesterday in the woods. My brother, Karl, has got Jodie, or someone, Mum's got Dad, and I am alone. All I have are my pets. No human'".

Within weeks of attending Pippa's funeral I visited a woman in hospital who had been anorexic for twenty-five years. She had had countless admissions to the psychiatric ward but the relevant issues had never been addressed. In the same hospital a psychiatrist confessed that she did not believe that recovery from anorexia was even possible.

In the midst of the world's negativity, we can wonder whether there is hope. But unless sufferers, family, friends and those in the caring professions hold on to full recovery we might as well give up. And I am not prepared to write off a person, are you? There are plenty of people, and I am one of them, who are living proof that there is life after an eating disorder, a life that is no longer driven by food and weight obsessions. True recovery will have involved experiencing the winter, where what is seen on the outside is removed to expose what lies underneath. With spring new life emerges. No one can truly survive and not have grown, blossoming into greater beauty. Life, at times, may still be painful, but there is now the ability to embrace the pain and not run away from it.

*Helena Wilkinson*
*Farnham, 1993*

# PART 1
## THE CRY FROM THE HEART

# 1 | UNTANGLING THE WEB

'I guess it began in childhood'. Bryony sat on the edge of the chair, her beautiful young face strained with inner torment. 'I was an only child and my mum was an alcoholic. Dad was very passive. I started infant school and was sexually abused.

'Mum became worse and I badly needed cuddles. I felt that there was something horribly wrong with me because she wanted to drink more than she wanted to be with me. Every evening she crashed out on the floor in a drunken haze and Dad just stepped over her. I was always covering up for Mum and pretending I didn't care when she forgot birthdays and Christmas. I used to buy my own presents so it wouldn't look bad when relatives visited.

'When I started work I was sexually harassed by my boss. He attempted to rape me and I left. I stopped eating as a way of denying that I was alive. I liked my new thin body; the cold, dead feeling numbed everything. Then I started to binge and vomit. Apart from work I'd only go out to buy food. To my horror I was admitted to a psychiatric hospital. The high calorie drink felt like "rape in a glass" and being weighed naked was a violation.

'Eventually I was referred to a therapeutic community. The approach was completely different: how much I weighed was not the priority. At first I felt panicky as I realised that I was going to look at the deep-seated pain and not just hide behind my food plans. Responsibility for my recovery was given back to me and I began to fight for myself. I am learning to express my thoughts and show my feelings. I have cried once or twice and hope that when I leave I will be able to shout, scream, cry or laugh. I have discovered that I am loved, and able to love in return. I feel like I matter at last'.

## The struggle

Many people struggle with food and weight. For Bryony the problem was classed as anorexia. Others battle with bulimia or compulsive eating. Some may be aware that they have a problem but it doesn't quite fit into one of the three eating disorders. Slotting into a specific category, although sometimes helpful, is not what is important. What is of value on reading this book is that people hold on to what is useful for *them* as individuals. The book by no means provides all the answers, but I hope it will encourage readers to look at the underlying issues. My guess is that a fair number of readers will pick up this book feeling relieved that eating disorders are being addressed but, as they read on, will find themselves experiencing pain. The temptation will be to shut the pages and run. Before doing so, consider an old therapeutic adage: 'The only way out is through'. If reading does become uncomfortable, I would advise you to discard what is not relevant for *you*, face what is true, and communicate how you feel to someone who cares.

\*    \*    \*

In order for a diagnosis of anorexia and bulimia to be made certain features must be present.

## Anorexia

a.   Body weight 15 percent or more lower than normal for age and height.
b.   Intense fear of gaining weight or becoming fat, even though underweight.
c.   Disturbance in the way in which body weight, size or

shape is experienced, e.g. claiming to 'feel fat' even when emaciated.

d. In females, absence of at least three consecutive menstrual cycles when otherwise expected to occur.[1]

## Bulimia

a.   Recurrent episodes of binge eating (rapid consumption of a large amount of food in a short time).

b.   A feeling of lack of control over eating behaviour during the eating binges.

c.   The person regularly engages in either self-induced vomiting, use of laxatives or diuretics, strict dieting or fasting, or vigorous exercise in order to prevent weight gain.

d.   A minimal average of two binge eating episodes a week for a least three months.

e.   Persistent over-concern with body shape and weight.[2]

Members of the caring professions may look at anorexia and bulimia slightly differently. Some will consider that a person can suffer from both anorexia and bulimia at the same time. Others will divide anorexics into restricting anorexics (who only use not eating to lose weight) and bingeing anorexics (who also have periods of bingeing and vomiting or taking laxatives/diuretics). Some will class people who binge and take laxatives/diuretics, use fasting and exercise but do not vomit, as bulimic. Others would argue that bulimics overeat 'in order to make themselves sick',[3] indicating that to be classed as bulimic the person must self-induce vomiting.

My feelings are that there are restricting anorexics and bingeing anorexics who are *underweight*, and that a bulimic is a person who binges and vomits and remains at a *near normal weight*. This allows a compulsive eater to be seen as someone who has bingeing sessions or who 'grazes' on food most of the day and does not vomit. She may be overweight or, if she engages in periods of obsessive dieting, her weight may be near normal. But not all overweight people are compulsive eaters. A low metabolic rate, lack of exercise and some medical conditions can result in obesity.

## Triumphant starvation

The anorexic carefully controls what she eats. There are 'acceptable' and 'unacceptable' foods. 'Unacceptable' foods start off as high calorie foods and later become any carbohydrates or fats, and in some cases anything other than certain vegetables, salads or fruits.

Although the anorexic declares that she is not hungry, apart from periods of loss of appetite through depression or the effects of prolonged starvation, she is very hungry. She feels triumphant in not giving in to the sensation; when she does give in she is filled with self-disgust at her weakness. Isobel found that as she ate 'every mouthful was like pushing something vile into a container that had no space'. It is not that the anorexic doesn't like food but that she fears losing control and over-indulging. In fact, she is fascinated by food and spends hours reading cookery books and preparing meals for other people. There is intense panic if she has to eat more than she has planned.

When the anorexic sets out on her cutting back on eating she seems no different from anyone else who is dieting, but there is a subtle difference. For the dieter who is not heading in the direction of anorexia dieting is *one* part of her life and she diets to achieve physical attractiveness. For the anorexic dieting is her *whole* life and she diets to achieve mastery over self. The anorexic is also unable to be realistic about the effects of food, considering that eating a small piece of cake will cause her to put on a lot of weight even if she has eaten nothing all day.

Emphasis from the media that slimness results in success, or comments in connection with a person's weight, can lead to the decision to diet. Alternatively, the potential anorexic may continue to diet following weight loss during an illness. But dieting itself is not the *cause* of anorexia. Certain factors will already have put the person in a position of making her susceptible, such as personality, family background, desire for perfection and suppression of feelings. As she diets and discovers that it gives her a sense of achievement she is motivated to keep losing weight when others would have stopped. She feels uneasy and bloated when she has eaten – the emptier she feels the better.

## Ever downward spiral

The anorexic has a fear of weighing more than a certain weight (which is below average for her age and height). Sometimes anorexics believe in a 'magical' weight at which they consider that everything will be OK. When they achieve this weight and discover that nothing has changed they set another 'goal'. The pattern continues in an ever downward spiral. The anorexic weighs herself frequently; the scales consistently tell lies. When she looks in the mirror a huge flabby figure stares back at her and her face, filled with horror, gives away how much she detests the sight. She examines herself with great precision. Her hands glide over her body searching for sharp angular bones. As her fingers feel the hardness she is reassured, but it is still not quite good enough.

Not eating causes restlessness and over-activity. The anorexic wakes early in the morning ready to move. She develops frantic exercise programmes pushing her body to physical extremes. Exercise involves discipline and not only keeps her weight down but rids her of guilt and helps her to feel warmer without eating more. As with fasting, excessive exercise releases endorphins in the brain which causes the anorexic to feel 'high'.

Soon the anorexic begins to develop rituals dictating that things must be done in a certain order at a certain time. She becomes obsessive and often very concerned with cleanliness and tidiness. There is intense self-hatred when she fails to keep the harsh rules she has imposed. She can't allow herself to enjoy life and feels guilty when she does. Her body must not rest. She denies herself things which others consider to be the basics of life, calling them luxuries. She is hard-working, determined and very competitive. She buries herself in work, partly because achievement is so important and partly so that she has less time to eat. She becomes obsessively concerned with what other people think of her.

## Facing the facts

Children, as well as teenagers and adults, can suffer from anorexia although early signs in children tend to be slightly different. These may be repeated complaints of feeling full, feeling sick, having a tummy ache or experiencing difficulty in swallowing. Anorexia and bulimia also occur in men, but only account for about 10 per cent of the cases. Male anorexia differs little from female anorexia, except men tend to put more emphasis on exercise than on dieting, and hormonal changes mean that they no longer have penile erections. Part of the explanation as to why more women than men suffer is that women tend to direct their pain towards themselves whilst men more easily turn their pain towards other people. The media have also dictated that, in general, a woman's self-image relates to her body and a man's to his work.

It can be hard for family and friends to detect anorexia early. The sufferer knows the calorie content of foods better than most people, and many tricks are devised to give the impression that she eats more than she actually does. She denies having a problem, distorts the truth and covers her emaciated body in layers of clothes.

Starvation causes irritability and selfishness and as the anorexic struggles with inner pain, and pushes against other people's control, she undergoes a personality change. A once-compliant, gentle and intelligent person becomes difficult and deceitful. As she withdraws from people her isolation grows along with her unhappiness. Elizabeth, who was anorexic from her early teens, remembers the difference between what *she* was experiencing and what *other people* were seeing. 'I felt as though I was screaming inside – yet to everyone else I was becoming more and more withdrawn'.

The anorexic's family and friends tell her how she is destroying their lives and that she is manipulative. Her extreme sensitivity takes in each word, twisting it round in her mind with piercing self-hatred. She decides to shut people out even further.

The lower her weight the more impaired the anorexic's thinking becomes. Everything is seen in very black and white terms. She also loses much of her ability to be creative, expressive, imaginative, and to handle challenging situations:

> "Being with even quite a small group of people will be too much to cope with, and a situation the sufferer will increasingly avoid. The number of interactions that take place in a group readily confuses and overwhelms people whose intellectual capacity is impaired by starvation. Every aspect of life will need to be totally predictable and organised well in advance".[4]

As her weight drops her drooping frame is no more than skin and bone. Shoulder blades and hip bones protrude. Her eyes are sunken and her skin pale. Her hands and feet feel perpetually cold and appear slightly purple due to poor circulation. On her arms, legs, back and face she may begin to develop a fine downy hair, her body's attempt to stay warm. She is frequently constipated, her skin is dry and her hair brittle. Her body is frail to hold. It is painful for her to sit on hard surfaces and as she walks she feels her knee bones rub together. She begins to feel dizzy and, at times, passes out. Her blood pressure is low and her heart rate slow. She begins to speak on one note. If the weight loss is severe and prolonged her bones will be like those of a much older person and she will develop osteoporosis. Her legs and ankles may become puffy and swollen.

Despite her physical symptoms the anorexic carries out her rituals with determination. Other people notice that she is irritable and inflexible; she fears that if she lets go she will be faced with a surge of indulgence and agonising feelings. When people try to convince her that she is not well she sees it as a threat. Initially she feels superior, as she is able to refuse food when others give in. But this feeling of superiority rarely lasts.

Anorexia usually develops in the teenage years whereas bulimia tends to affect people who are slightly older. Bulimics are also more outgoing, expressive and impulsive than anorexics. It is not uncommon for an anorexic to go on to develop bulimia as she begins to let go of her control and to face, but not be able to hold onto, her feelings.

## Dying on the inside

The bulimic only *appears* to be confident; underneath she doubts herself and feels that she has failed. Her moods swing from despair to elation in a very short time. Charlotte looked healthy enough, she could laugh and smile, but on the inside she was dying. 'I was standing watching my friends enjoying themselves – watching but never fully joining in'.

At times the bulimic can eat a normal meal without getting rid of the food. On other occasions she feels overcome by guilt and chooses to induce vomiting. She may starve herself all day and then crave food in the evening or raid the fridge in the middle of the night. The foods she buys for bingeing are those which she usually avoids eating. Sometimes her desperation to binge and vomit is so great that she doesn't care what she eats. Raw vegetables, raw meat, dry cereal, sweet, savoury and half-cooked food are all crammed in, one after the other, at great speed. Packets are ripped open and there is an urgency in her eating. The amount of calories consumed in one binge can be equal to what most people would eat in ten days, sometimes more. Her bingeing and vomiting may occur only twice a week or twenty times in a day. However frequently the pattern occurs it is usually her need for release of tension, rather than hunger, which drives her to binge.

After her binge she feels heavy, her stomach is distended as though it may burst open. She is hot and sweaty. She forces herself to vomit until she is sure that all the food has gone and she can return to a comforting state of emptiness. She feels tired and numb, but relaxed. Her bingeing and vomiting concludes with carefully cleaning the bathroom, tidying up and washing herself. Often after this she collapses exhausted. She must not let anyone know about her dreadful secret.

Sometimes the bulimic feels disgusted by what she does and vows that she will *never* do it again. In a fit of desperation she forgets her promise and repeats the cycle. At other times there is a love-hate relationship: whilst she is disgusted that she could be capable of such behaviour, there is also a sense of excitement.

Bulimia is very hard for family and friends to detect. Large amounts of food disappearing , money struggles, increased eating without weight gain, visiting the bathroom regularly after meals, spending a long time in the bathroom, and fluctuations in weight can all be signs.

The bulimic may appear to have a puffy face due to swelling of the salivary glands, and be prone to throat infections. Perpetual vomiting can cause the oesophagus to bleed, and the enamel on her teeth to erode. A disturbance in the balance of electrolytes (potassium, sodium, magnesium and calcium, etc.) affects both the bulimic and the anorexic. This can cause muscle weakness, numbness, kidney failure, and an erratic heartbeat. In a small number of people it can result in epileptic fits or heart failure. Anaemia or a decreased white blood cell count can also occur.

Some bulimics and anorexics resort to taking laxatives to get rid of the guilt of eating or to 'cleanse' themselves. The body becomes used to relying on the laxatives and they cease to be as effective, forcing the sufferer to increase the amount. In addition, she may use diuretics to get rid of water and so feel lighter. Abuse of laxatives can result in abdominal pain, nausea, muscle spasms, and chest pain. The weight loss is nearly all fluid and yet the sufferer feels panic-stricken if forced to give up her addiction.

When anyone with an eating disorder becomes desperate enough for food or laxatives, but cannot afford them, they may turn to shoplifting. In addition, they may alter their behaviour in ever more harmful ways. Drug and alcohol abuse is not uncommon in people with eating disorders, but it is more often the bulimic who turns to this additional form of addiction.[5] Self-harm is also more common in the bulimic. Cutting or burning herself is frequently misunderstood as attention-seeking but usually it is done in secret and is a way of releasing tension and suppressed feelings, or a way of enabling the sufferer to feel 'alive'. Sometimes people can become addicted to the shot of adrenalin which self-harm causes. Other forms of self-harm which are adopted by all types of sufferers are: bruising; biting; scratching; pulling out hair; purposely getting very cold. Overdoses which are not serious suicide attempts are also taken as an expression of self-harm.

Until recently, when people talked about eating disorders, anorexia and bulimia came to mind; compulsive eating was rarely acknowledged as a problem which arises out of emotional struggles. It has also been seen as the most undesirable of the three eating disorders. Anorexics are sometimes admired for attaining incredible control, bulimics envied for being able to eat and remain slim, but compulsive eaters are more often seen merely as weak willed. For the compulsive eater the desire to eat is overwhelming, but usually this is not as a result of physical hunger.

## Fantasising a feast

Compulsive eating, as with any eating disorder, is a form of addiction. Naomi has been a sufferer for several years. 'I have a mental image of myself as a shoal of piranha fish in a feeding frenzy. I even sob as I stuff yet more food into my already sore mouth'. To the compulsive eater, food means either overeating or dieting. It is also something about which she fantasises a great deal and which offers her comfort.

When the compulsive eater gives an account of what she has eaten that day she frequently fails to include certain foods. Some sufferers subconsciously believe that if they eat whilst standing up, driving or walking it 'doesn't count'. She doesn't usually like looking at herself in the mirror. 'Women in therapy often say they experience or see themselves as though there is no connection between the head and the body. The neck is usually the dividing line'.[6]

Despite the fact that over 50 per cent of women are size 14+ (UK sizes), the media usually portray size 10 or 12 as 'average', which puts women under enormous pressure to feel that they must lose weight. The compulsive eater may set out on a diet because of the pressure to be slim, but dieting feels like imprisonment. As she attempts to return to normal eating she often finds herself making up for those things of which she has been deprived. She experiences a deep hole inside her which is carved out by pain. It hurts for it to be empty but there never seems to be enough food to fill it. One of the deepest fears of the compulsive eater is being hungry. Felicity admitted that if she is going out to a party where there is food she still eats a meal before she goes. 'I also eat when I am not hungry in case I am hungry in a couple of hours'.

The overweight compulsive eater often feels a freak. She laughs it off on the outside, appearing to be full of fun, but crumples on the inside. She may find eating in front of other people uncomfortable, convinced that they think she should be dieting. Other people may assume that she is someone who is not bothered about matters such as achieving the ideal figure.

The compulsive eater is so haunted by food that she might deliberately walk home a certain way in order to pass a food store. She makes excuses as she buys large quantities of provisions. 'I'll buy eight pastries for the kids', she reasons – only the kids never see the pastries as half are devoured on the way home and the remainder throughout the day. She eats guiltily and with speed, not really enjoying what she is eating, afraid that others might 'catch her'. Buying one item of food, especially sweet food, frequently leads to her buying more and more.

There are physical consequences for the compulsive eater, and not just because of being overweight. Current research is showing that people who diet and then regain their weight, and repeat the pattern over and over, are far more susceptible to gallstones. Overweight people are more likely to develop diabetes, raised blood cholesterol and to suffer from strokes and heart attacks.

Many compulsive eaters say that it would be harder to give up sweet foods than to give up some of their closest friends. The compulsion is so strong that even feeling physically full rarely stops them eating. For Shelley each day became a nightmare. 'My whole life revolved around when I could get my next "fix" of food'.

Throughout an eating disorder, whether anorexia,

bulimia or compulsive eating, the sufferer is communicating some very powerful messages. In the next few chapters we will be exploring these.

# 2 | *RUNNING FROM LIFE*

Anorexia is not really the problem, but rather a way of coping with a whole series of problems. For various reasons the potential anorexic feels unsafe, and she discovers that through not eating and pursuing thinness she is in a better position to handle her world. Life is seen as frightening, full of situations, experiences and responsibilities with which she feels she can't cope.

The type of person who develops anorexia is usually someone who lacks confidence, feels self-conscious and finds change difficult. Traumatic events may not necessarily have happened to her – life itself feels traumatic. Tiffany experienced just that. It hurt her that she hurt other people. She hated herself and was in great emotional pain. She considered that she had made a mess of her life. 'I feel as if people are looking at me all the time and talking and laughing at me. I'm so self-conscious that I cannot even look someone in the eye. I am extremely lonely and feel as if no one wants to be my friend. When people talk to me I never know what to say to them. I feel so insecure and immature'. Sadly, Tiffany felt there was no way out other than to take her own life. Her final note said that others would be better off without her. Although Tiffany despised herself and felt clumsy, her brother described her as someone who loved selflessly, gave of herself to everybody, never asked for anything in return, and was always there for other people.

## Escaping pain
The pain from which the anorexic is trying to escape can be related to anything, including bullying at school,

break-up of a friendship, or the death of someone close. When things go wrong the anorexic starves herself, but this is not a loss of appetite as when someone is depressed or grieving. Anorexia actually *takes the place* of grieving and prevents the sufferer from feeling. There is a desperate need to hide the part of herself which has already been, and may continue to be, wounded. By withdrawing and concentrating on food and weight the anorexic puts herself in a position of not forming deep relationships, reducing the chances of criticism and rejection.

The anorexic doesn't know what to do with pain or ordinary feelings such as neediness, anger, frustration, jealousy and vulnerability. John Bradshaw considers that the anorexic *renounces* her emotions by refusing to eat, and that food seems to equal feelings.[1] She believes that she should have only 'nice' feelings. As she discovers that it is not possible to have only 'nice' feelings she begins to look upon all feelings with disdain. The cost is that, in ridding herself of feelings, she comes across as lacking vitality and other people find it hard to relate to her.

To one struggling with crushing emotional pain, a loss of feeling can seem very attractive. Not eating produces an addictive 'high', which masks the emptiness. I remember as a young teenager at boarding school sinking into deep depression, following years of emotional and physical hurts. As I developed anorexia my depression began to lift. My anorexic behaviour gave me a goal to work towards and it shut the pain of other people out. Once the pattern sets in, other problems appear to diminish. In the early stages of the illness I had never felt better – I was attaining a level of willpower that none of my classmates even came near. The lower my weight the more remote the world seemed. I began to feel numb. I did not have to think about, or cope with, normal experiences and emotions. The only feelings I had were in relation to food and weight. I was like a piece of china –

perfectly fragile and something which people would be very careful not to knock or break.

## Hiding conflict

The behaviour patterns of the anorexic distract her from confronting her true feelings. Since she has usually been brought up in a family which is not comfortable with expressing conflict or anger, she feels that these cannot be openly directed at anyone. Anger is pushed down and not eating becomes her one means of expressing her anger. She may be hurt, disappointed and angry with those close to her but, because she does not know how to resolve conflict, facing these feelings is too dangerous and she feels that she must destroy them. The anorexic is rarely aware that she is angry for any reason other than being made to eat.

If anger has not been allowed to be expressed it becomes an alienated part of the person. The person feels shame whenever she is angry. This part of her must be disowned or severed. Blocking off the emotional energy of anger, she becomes a people-pleaser. All her feelings, needs and drives are bound by shame. When the shame has been completely internalised, nothing about her feels OK – she feels flawed and inferior. She turns her eyes inwards and scrutinises every minute detail of behaviour, creating a tormenting self-conscience. With parts of her severed and alienated there is a sense of unreality; of never quite belonging.[2]

Lauren was in her teens when she developed anorexia. She had been through years of bullying and abuse as a young child but there was no one she could talk to about her experiences. If ever she expressed her anger at home it came out as being manipulative or moody. Most of the time she covered up her feelings or withdrew. Her parents found anger and conflict hard to live with. It was as though they could not cope with anger within themselves and so would not allow it in their children. They did not ban anger or conflict but the level of anxiety would rise whenever either was expressed. 'It's not that conflict didn't exist in our house', said Lauren, 'but it always stayed in the atmosphere and was never talked about'. Instead of thinking she was angry Lauren believed that she was naughty. If she was with children of her own age she felt 'different'. By the time she developed anorexia she found that she could not handle anger and conflict in either herself or other people. Even a difference of opinion felt frightening and as if she were failing to conform to other people's wishes, so would not be liked.

## Seeking identity

The sufferer finds herself in a great deal of conflict over who she is and where she fits in with her friends. Her uncertainty over identity can have arisen for a number of reasons: she may be searching for the meaning of life; be struggling with being a twin; have come from a different culture; be wanting to find her roots, having been adopted. More commonly the issue over identity has a connection with the way her family relates, expecting her to be a part of the way *they* see and do things rather than someone able to form her own opinions.

'Children cannot know who they are without reflective mirrors ... Parents who are shut down emotionally cannot mirror and affirm their children's emotions.[3] To mirror and affirm an emotion is, for example, to say to a child when she is upset, 'I sense that you are hurting. It's OK to cry'. The opposite is to attempt to take the pain away without understanding how she is feeling, or to impress on her that she shouldn't feel that way. If in addition to lack of mirroring and affirming of emotions there is neglect of needs, abuse, or unhealthy over-involvement, the result is a loss of identity and feelings of abandonment.

A loss of identity can also develop when a child is too controlled by another person or made to feel that she must become what someone else wants her to be, without any chance to experiment for herself. A typical situation for the anorexic is that she may not, for fear of losing approval, have been through times of rebelling, or choosing clothes, friends or music that her parents don't like. Gemma, before developing anorexia, had little sense of who she was. 'I felt that I was being poured by vague and wondering hands into a mould into which I did not fit'. For Gemma the conflict over identity seemed to be one which could never be resolved. Anorexia created a form of identity for her and gave her a stronger sense of being in charge of her own life, which felt better than its being managed by her parents.

Anorexia often starts at a time in a person's life when she is questioning who she is, whether she really matters and what life is all about. There is an intensity in the questions being asked and she has a panic-stricken feeling that there are *no* answers. 'Yes, she is damaging herself; yes, she could die or do herself irreparable harm. But the alternative for her is to give in and be nothing'.[4]

The lack of individuality in anorexics extends to friendships:

> "Quite often there has been a whole series of friendships, but with only one friend at a time. With each new friend anorexics will develop different interests and a different personality. They conceive of themselves as blanks who just go along with what the friend enjoys and wants to do. The idea that they have their own individuality to contribute to a friendship never occurs to them".[5]

Anorexics hope that somehow they will just become a part of the friendship without having to do anything to make it work. Yet they also fear that they will end up feeling disappointed with their friends, or the friendship won't be quite right or good enough.

A problem in friendships can also develop if the

sufferer finds it difficult to distinguish between closeness and being taken over, and between space and rejection. Marilyn Lawrence, a therapist, recalls the significance of these issues with one of her clients, Anna:

> "Anna wondered how she could love someone and still want to be away from them; how someone could love her and still love other people; how she could want to be close to someone at one time and not at another; how she could want to be known completely and yet still retain her privacy. It seemed irresolvable. To be close meant to be so close, so intimate, that there was, there could be, no distance: she was at one with the other person. All distance was painful and, in fact, perceived as persecuting. To be absolutely close was the only place of safety; it was home. If she could not have that, then she would be cut off. Food became a metaphor. As an anorexic she cut off from her hunger and her desire for food; she simply ate the same food at the same time every day. So too with her desire for closeness. She cut herself off from other people so that she didn't have to examine what she felt or what she wanted or *if* she wanted it".[6]

## Declaring independence

A crisis over independence arises out of the fact that other people have defined how the potential sufferer *should* be. Lack of individuality leads to over-submissiveness, non-assertiveness and difficulty in making decisions or forming opinions. It is hard for the anorexic to know what she wants and doesn't want because mostly other people have indicated what she *ought* to want. Some of the rules and rituals she creates concerning what she will eat, and when, enable her to feel that she is making choices and decisions about preferences.

Although the child who becomes anorexic wants to conform to her family's closeness, politeness and freedom from conflict she also wants her independence. In controlling her food and weight she is making a statement about independence. Yet, in regressing to a childlike state physically she is showing that she cannot cope with independence and wants to be looked after. It is not unusual to find an anorexic woman in her twenties who says she wants to leave home but when she is helped to find a place of her own returns to her parents. She is unable to sustain being on her own.

The way the different sexes are treated in the developing years affects their struggle with identity and independence and may have a connection with the reason more women than men suffer from anorexia:

> "Little girls, more than little boys, are brought up to be 'good'. Passivity and compliance are qualities which are valued highly in girls whereas in boys a certain amount of resistance and rebellion is regarded as healthy. Compliant, passive and unselfish daughters may make for a tranquil family life; such a training however does not lead to a smooth passage to independence!"[7]

The anorexic has usually not been brought up in an environment where she has been able to be silly or make a mess and still feel accepted. She has rarely experienced what it is like to be hurt and retreat into embracing arms without over-reaction or over-protectiveness. Being with people who are both silly and tease her feels extremely painful. Peer groups involve both silliness and teasing, but they are also an essential part of learning about life and independence.

The potential anorexic stands on the edge of the group, not feeling that she belongs or considering herself 'not normal'. Peter Lambley comments that, for the anorexic, 'not normal' means having the basis of her creativity and energy cut away and pushed into empty, superficial rituals which leave her lonely and disgruntled. She hates herself for needing attention, for whining and for being a nuisance. She goes on protesting but feels bad and ugly:

> "There is no physical contact, no emotionality, no challenge, no childishness, no outside contact. The anorexic girl senses these things and learns (while her peers are busy enjoying life) that all these needs are signs of inadequacy or weakness. To the loneliness is added a deep sense of guilt and hurt: a massive and growing nausea and self-disgust. And no way to solve it."[8]

## Fearing responsibility

Responsibility is often seen as requiring a level of self-confidence and assertiveness which the sufferer feels she doesn't have. She experiences the expectations of not only her parents but other people as too demanding. Not having been encouraged to make her own decisions, she passively waits for others to take the initiative. The thought of initiating anything or having to make decisions can create feelings of deep panic or pain. Jill Welbourne and Joan Purgold, in their work with the anorexic's indecisiveness, have noticed

> "... that an inherited conflict of values passed on to the sufferer by her parents has been an important factor. Typically her father will have shown her by his example how important it is to be independent and think for herself and by her own efforts get ahead and achieve results. During the same formative years her mother will have been teaching her to show consideration for other people and impressing on her how important it is not to be greedy or selfish".[9]

The struggle with making decisions can seem like torture. Even deciding what clothes to buy can create unbearable anxiety:

> "It is not so much a question of not knowing what she wants; she doesn't of course but that is the lesser problem, the major problem is that she does not know what she *ought* to want. For most people, need determines choice but what the anorexic may need barely concerns her since she is usually convinced that she deserves and therefore should have – nothing".[10]

The anorexic tends to be sensitive and a deep thinker who takes things very seriously and personally. She feels responsible for the whole world and is burdened by events around her when other teenagers are too busy talking about dating and fashion to notice. Contact with the world may have been minimal in her family, or the world may have been talked about as somewhere fraught with danger, from chemicals in foods to rapists in the streets. When she is faced with the prospect of stepping outside her home, it is like putting a foot into the jungle: she feels exposed and not sure what's going to attack her first. She reasons it is safer to lock herself into her own little world, even if at times it feels like a prison.

## Desiring perfection

The desire to overcome that which is not 'nice' and to attain purity is very strong in the anorexic. Marilyn Lawrence and Mira Dana see this as a quest for *moral perfection*.[11] The meeting of ordinary needs such as hunger and comfort is regarded as a sign of moral failure. Anything which falls below the anorexic's standard is 'bad'. Unlike most people who, in viewing themselves or life experiences, have a sliding scale of varying degrees of goodness and badness, the anorexic has only two points – 'totally good' or 'utterly bad'.

Perfection is shown in high standards for herself and in the way she relates to others. Her determination and drive, which are very strong, can be both positive and negative. These usually mean that the anorexic achieves well but also that when most people would give up she will still be pushing herself, resulting in unnecessary pressure. Being average means not being good enough and feeling like 'a nothing'. The more she strives to be perfect, the more she feels people will accept her, and acceptance by others is very important. Even before developing the eating disorder she was the kind of person who would always seek to please others and was in need of much affirmation.

The anorexic's striving for perfection becomes concentrated on the body but in reality relates to the whole of her life. Everything she does needs to be working towards a goal. The difficulty is that whatever level of perfection the anorexic achieves she still lives under a thick cloud of the fear of failure. She is afraid of not living up to what she thinks is expected of her. There is a constant dread of being discovered not perfect. However low her weight is, it is never low enough because she can still sense that there is an unacceptable part of her needing to be eradicated.

A part of the path to perfection is the need to achieve academically. Anorexics are usually intelligent girls whose parents or teachers, in their keenness to see the young woman reach her potential, have put more stress on academic standards than on valuing her for who she is. Sometimes the anorexic has an intelligent sibling, and despite her own intelligence she constantly stands in her brother's/sister's shadow, always feeling second best. Starving herself gives her the sense that she can achieve in a way in which others so often fail.

## Keeping control
The main purpose behind anorexia is control. Anorexia gives a sense of power in a life that has known the struggle of powerlessness. Whether that powerlessness has been through having a controlling parent figure, abuse, an intimidating sibling, or maltreatment at school

for example, there exists the need, now, to feel in control and never experience that terrible sense of powerlessness again.

The sufferer's harsh judgements of herself, her low self-esteem and her extreme sensitivity leave her vulnerable to the control of other people. Her experience is of being pressured by everyone with whom she comes into contact. Other people's needs, feelings and expectations automatically become obligations upon her. Because she feels there is no way of resolving the conflict which these needs and expectations create, she feels trapped and confused.[12] Her answer is to try to take control for herself. There soon becomes a battle for control in the anorexic family: the parents want to control their child and she wants to control her own life. If she can't control her circumstances she controls herself within those circumstances. Not eating becomes the only way she knows how to take control.

Loss of control is considered as 'failure' and greatly feared. The control is not merely in connection with food and weight but over every area of life. There exists the fear that the minute the slightest control is lost, all control will disappear and she will be forced to the depths of self-indulgence. Guilt acts as a deadly reminder that indulgence, of even the smallest amount, is the ultimate 'sin'; and 'giving in' is a sign of complete and utter uselessness.

Losing weight is proof to the anorexic that she is able to exert will-power over the less desirable things in life, such as indulgence and feelings. It is a way of declaring that she does not need anything, especially nourishment and people. Yet inside she is crying out for the very things she is rejecting.

I am poor and helpless,
   and I have lost all hope.
I am fading away
   like an evening shadow;
I am tossed aside
   like a crawling insect.
I have gone without eating,
   until my knees are weak,
   and my body is bony.

Please help me, Lord God!
Come and save me
   because of your love.
Psalm 109:22-24, 26 CEV

# 3 | *HIDING A MONSTER*

In endeavouring to provide an explanation for the bulimic's behaviour, Mira Dana and Marilyn Lawrence bring out a valid point. They effectively say that the taking in of food and the vomiting of it out can be understood properly only if these are seen as one unified action. Together they reveal a variety of meanings and represent what is going on in the emotional world of the bulimic.[1]

## Conflicting images

The bulimic is trying hard to take control of her life but is also in a great deal of conflict. She wants to present herself as someone who is strong and yet inside she feels needy and emotionally hungry. The conflict is in connection with her worth and with her relating to others. A socially competent and successful appearance covers up a person full of doubts, inadequacies, fears and an aching aloneness.

At the time she developed bulimia Charlotte's natural personality was bubbly, light-hearted and adventurous. But inside it was as if this person were lost. She was wrapped in fear, loneliness and an inner isolation. 'It felt like I was two people: one was capable, strong and intelligent; the other was vulnerable, weak and needing protecting. They conflicted. The little child in me wouldn't allow the adult to grow up and the adult was desperately trying to be that little child'.

There is a split between the part of the bulimic which is very much in control and is a coper and the part which is dependent and a non-coper. This is something with which most people struggle to a certain degree but in the bulimic appears to be accentuated. She feels ashamed of the non-coping part of herself which she tries to shut away from others. Only as the sufferer looks back on her experience is she able to see the role that bulimia has played in her life. The nature of the illness is one of covering up. It is about hiding the truth, hiding feelings, hiding food. Everything is done in secret – the eating, the vomiting, the tears.

Many recovered bulimics say that subconsciously they always felt that there was something terribly wrong with them – that they were both bad and nasty. 'No one must see the pain', Hilary explained, 'if they do it means they will know that inside there is a bad person who does not deserve approval'. Throughout her illness Hilary had worked hard to keep the pain and the 'bad' part of herself carefully locked in the bathroom where she performed her shameful act. The other part was still able to go on relating at an intellectual level, and continued to be admired by others. For Hilary, and many other sufferers, the secrecy only compounds the feeling of badness. Safety, for all these people, is found in familiarity and lack of vulnerability. To observe the behaviour of the bulimic – the desperate craving, the rapidity with which food is often consumed, and the secretiveness – is to see that the conflict is 'about having a clean, neat, good, un-needy appearance which conceals behind it a messy needy bad part, which must be hidden away'.[2]

Sometimes the vomiting is seen by the bulimic as a punishment for the gap which exists between the aspect of her she shows to the world and the aspect she keeps hidden. Michelle battled with bulimia for eleven years:

> "Other people thought that I always seemed so together, fit, healthy and happy. But often I was very low, felt misunderstood, unloved, and suffered from exhaustion. Bulimia feels like being trapped, like

living in a shell out of which there is no escape. It feels very much as though a monster lives inside, who has all the control and is impossible to get rid of. As well as feeling shut off from the world, inside there is a great emptiness which does not seem to be able to be filled".

The worse the illness becomes the bigger the monster grows and the greater the fear that one day it may burst out of her skin for the whole world to see.

In addition to being emotionally symbolic, the bulimic pattern can be a way of physically releasing tension brought about through inner conflict, family problems, loneliness, stress, anxiety and depression.

## Shifting relating

By consuming enormous amounts of food the bulimic is saying 'I am desperately needy'. By vomiting it all out she proclaims 'I reject it all. I am terrified of actually having any of my needs met'. She can show a similar attitude in her relationships. She will often find herself driven into a relationship by her emotional needs but later puts an end to it because of fear.[3]

Life for the bulimic feels like a vicious circle. She wants to achieve high standards, she wants perfection in relationships, but she feels it is impossible to maintain these standards. She binges instead. Just as the bulimic feels out of control with food, so she can feel out of control in relationships and with spending money.

Underneath the bulimic's façade there exists a hollow aloneness and hunger to be cared for. But she is afraid that once she allows people to touch the part of her which longs to be treasured they will be sucked into her vacuum of hunger. She feels so desperate and so much in need that if she dares to expose her desires too much she fears they will consume everything and everyone in sight. Once she allows her need for care and affirmation to rise to the surface it might take over, not only other people but her whole life. The bulimic usually reasons that she must only allow herself to experience these longings at certain moments – these are the occasions when she indulges in the world of food. Bingeing and vomiting is her one time of coming face to face with all she longs for, taking in more and more and more until full and satisfied and fit to burst. But she must only have all she longs for for a short while, then it must be emptied from her so that she can carry on with life, able and in control. It is hard for the bulimic to understand that everyone has longings at different moments, and that it's OK both to feel and admit to these longings. For her the feeling is dangerous and something which she is convinced will drive other people away. Some bulimics look upon their childlike longings with fierce hatred, feeling destructive and guilty and full of self-contempt.

Once a mistake has been made or the sufferer has been seen in a less than perfect light she feels that she must run. Friendships may be formed and dropped quite quickly. The pain inside is unbearable as she feels, yet again, that she must escape from someone with whom she considers she has 'blown it'. She often seeks relationships where there is a lack of commitment from the other person or with someone who does not give of themselves emotionally. She also finds it hard to be committed herself and may opt for short-term relationship or a relationship from which she can easily break away, making her feel safer. She repeats the same patterns, hoping to put a different ending to the story. Each time it fails it only adds to her desperation.

The bulimic is afraid of intimacy. She longs to feel close but dreads the thought that when other people get to know her they will discover the 'bad' part and be shocked. This means that she rarely experiences herself as deeply loved or nurtured by anyone. She lives in fear of the other person taking her over in a relationship, and of losing her identity. At other times she feels the urge to take control. Wanting to be cared for and then running before others have a chance *really* to get to know her creates a 'pull-push' relating. Michelle used to feel that she needed more space within her friendships, despite the fact that she craved company. 'The world seemed hostile, although I knew that it wasn't, that it was me who couldn't cope'. Not being able to deal with the struggles in friendships out in the open, or not recognising what is happening emotionally, means that the patterns are re-enacted in the bulimic's eating.

## Destroying love

The part of herself which the bulimic considers she needs to get rid of in her vomiting is

> "... the part of the self which is able to indicate what it is that the self really needs, feels, wants, likes, dislikes, yearns for. She has no access to this part of herself, and instead she becomes dominated by a series of 'oughts', 'shoulds' and 'musts': a set of external rules which she has carried with her since childhood and which bear little or no relation to what she wants or likes. Thoughts replace feelings; oughts, shoulds and shouldn'ts replace real emotional or physical preferences".[4]

Not only is the bulimic trying to create a perfect image, but she is also searching for a perfect love, a love which will enable her to feel differently about herself and her circumstances. Yet love in relationships never fully satisfies her. One man said of his bulimic girlfriend: 'She seems to treat relationships in the same way as she treats her food. She takes people in and then spits them out'. The more the bulimic becomes aware of the fact that she reacts in this way, the greater the pain she is in. Loving is experienced as destructive. To be loved by others is to risk destroying herself by letting the other person see the 'ugly' part of her, to be taken over by the other person or to lose control. To love others is to feel the desire to consume the other person, take total control and not allow them any breathing space.

The bulimic may be searching in adult relationships for what she felt she failed to find in her childhood relationships – a deep sense of being valued. Her hunger drives her to continue looking for it, but nothing ever seems to satisfy. Nothing can be held onto for any length of time:

> "Being bulimic provides her with a way of avoiding seeing and experiencing that yearning for love and approval and the emptiness and self-hatred perpetuated by the disappointment of not getting it. Overeating and vomiting fills up the empty space, while at the same time actively symbolising how impossible she finds it to take in and keep in anything good. The bulimia soon becomes for her the excuse, her reason, for not being loved".[5]

## Splitting feelings

The 'bad' part of the sufferer is seen as that which contains 'bad' feelings and weakness. These are feelings and experiences which she has been brought up to believe are not acceptable or must be kept hidden from other people, such as hostility, anger, sadness, sexual desire and neediness. Hilary came from a family where negative feelings were not allowed to be shown in case they took away the image of the 'perfect' family which was completely amicable:

> "I would cry myself to sleep most nights. If I did show anger I would become so out of control that my sister used to say I would become a murderer when I grew up. Any strong feelings I had which were 'bad' frightened me, so I ate to get rid of them. With the eating my

self-hatred grew as I knew that deep down I was wicked and that the 'good' exterior was just a cover up. My self-hatred also grew because each time I ate it confirmed I had no control over food".

The way in which some people deal with 'bad' feelings is to separate them from the 'good' feelings and not allow them to be part of the person they show to the outside world. Smiling depressives are an example of this: though deeply depressed they continue smiling, indicating that life is fine. The bulimic splits off her 'bad' feelings to such an extent that she reaches a point of believing that if she did not have bulimia she wouldn't have these feelings. She finds it extremely hard both to see and accept that negative feelings are a part of her, as they are of anyone.

The bulimia is a separate part of the sufferer which encapsulates 'the problems' in her life, like a bubble where all the unacceptable, hatred and feared aspects of herself are lodged. Her 'badness' is pushed away and centred on her bulimia. All her bad, needy, angry, dependent aspects become attached to the bulimia, so that they are not directly experienced. The bathroom is the one place she will allow her 'mess' to spill over.[6] Just as with the bulimia – when the sufferer vomits, creates a mess and then tidies up – so in everyday life, once any negative feelings come out or she makes a mistake, it is quickly dealt with and no one is any the wiser.

For Leanne suicidal thoughts, along with bingeing, purging and cutting herself were all attempts to get rid of the 'bad' inside. 'Bingeing pushed the bad down; purging was an attempt to get it out of myself. In cutting myself I believed that the bad would flow out along with the blood. Although some overdoses were obvious attempts on my life, others were ways to end the pain, the chaotic thoughts and the unacceptable feelings'.

Bulimia takes an enormous amount of energy. Energy

which would be used to express feelings is used to keep them down.

"Instead of feeling distress, she feels an uncontrollable appetite. These feelings throw her into chaos and she tries to satisfy herself by cramming food into her mouth. As soon as she has eaten and comes into touch with her needy, violent, devouring self, she is filled with guilt and feels an urgent desire to rid herself of what she has eaten. The end result of the bulimia, the eating and vomiting, is that the woman feels empty and entirely without needs. This is precisely the feeling she is seeking … In a limited way, bulimia achieves for her what she wants. The split-off, unwanted part of herself is contained in the symptom, leaving the rest of her life free from trouble and distress. The problem with this solution is that she has a continual sense of cheating, of achieving everything in a fraudulent way. Everything she actually does is undermined for her by the means she uses to achieve it."[7]

> My groaning has worn me out.
> At night my bed and pillow
>     are soaked with tears.
>
> I am lonely and troubled.
> Show that you care
>     and have pity on me.
> My awful worries keep growing.
>     Rescue me from sadness.
> Psalm 6:6; 25:16-17 CEV

# 4 | EASING THE PAIN

The attitude towards herself and towards other people often shows itself in the eating patterns of the compulsive eater. She is hungry for everything. By eating large quantities of food she can be expressing her need for more. Not just more food – more care, more understanding, more comfort, more time, more friends, more freedom, more of whatever she feels deprived of at the time. Shelley remembers her need for more and how, as a result, her experience of compulsive eating grew over the years:

"I believe that the desire for food as comfort started from the day I was born. I was a month premature and for the first forty-eight hours it was fifty/fifty as to whether I would live. As I was so small and weak I was fed regularly. I also spent the first four weeks in an incubator and had no physical contact with my mother. The only reassurance I had was food. My mother has since told me that when I was a child she constantly fed me. At four it was discovered that I had a hearing loss. I started school but found it difficult to make friends and to learn. I struggled through each day mostly feeling very lonely, sad and confused. Coming home to food was my only relief. My earliest memory of secret eating was when I was six. It became a challenge and thrill to steal biscuits and cakes and eat them without anyone finding out. I can see now that my childhood was frightening and I was unable to get my needs of love, reassurance and security met so I just withdrew into my world of food".

## Masking problems

Compulsive eating can be a lonely and depressing affair in which loving and relying on food can feel safer than loving and relying on people. Food is always close at hand when the sufferer is hurting – people are not. Food does not retaliate, challenge, have expectations or want anything in return – people might. Food helps to mask problems and to push down unwanted emotions. Compulsive eating can be used, without the person realising, to avoid the fact that her life is disappointing, comfort her when other people cause hurt, hide the vulnerable real part of her, or flee handling responsibility. Food is eaten to ease frustration and tension and to disguise insecurity.

The compulsive eater's solution to *any* pain or discomfort is food – to have something in the mouth and to fill up the gaping hole. When she is eating, the compulsive eater can feel warm, safe and strong. For a while, at least, she can forget about her hurts and about reality. She eats to anaesthetise painful feelings and may become agitated if anyone disturbs her special time with food. She believes that because food made her feel good the last time she was depressed it should do the same this time. She eats as a means of coping with uncomfortable feelings and in response to positive feelings. She eats when she is bored or if she if feeling out of control. There is hardly a situation or emotion that does not demand food. 'Both a sense of power and a sense of powerlessness are felt as hunger'.[1]

The compulsive eater may also turn to food when:

- she can't accomplish her too-high goals
- things don't go right
- people don't do what they should
- events don't run smoothly
- people don't like her behaviour

In short, the compulsive eater eats because the world doesn't operate the way it would it if were perfect. In addition she may:

• minimise her successes
• maximise her failures
• see only problems ahead
• blame others when she falls short[2]

## Seeking relief

One of the warning signs of compulsive eating is that sufferers 'have a low tolerance for "negative" feelings (anger, sadness, fear, etc.)'.[3] The answer to this for many people is instant relief; 'I hurt and so I must find something which will take that hurt away *now*'. Little else is more instant in providing comfort than sweet food, especially chocolate.

The patterns of seeking relief from negative feelings and experiences through food are often learned early in childhood. The child who was always given sweets as a pacifier when she hurt herself or to keep her quiet will, in adult life, easily turn to food for comfort. Part of her problem with comfort eating is simply a matter of relying on what she has known to work since she was very little. Being raised in an unhappy or an unhealthy home, where boundaries are not clearly set or a child has no sense of the ability to make choices and do things for herself, the person may grow up with the ache of emotional emptiness which she soon translates into pangs of physical emptiness. She finds it hard to perceive that pain is a part of life which will not always go when she wants it to, and that gratification, at times, may need to be deferred. She can also find it difficult to perceive that greater satisfaction can be found in relationship with God and with other people than with food.

It is not unusual for sufferers to come from homes where the parents gave their children food, or deprived them of it, for reasons that had no relation to the child's sensations of hunger. The parents might have struggled to show affection except by the gift of food, or it may have been offered to distract the child, even tranquillise her, by an otherwise occupied mother. Such mothers will have deprived the child of the ability to learn for herself whether she is truly hungry. When the child grows up she will have suffered two fundamental gaps in her education: not being able to recognise real hunger and being deprived of a feeling of independence.[4]

When in pain or under stress the natural human reaction is to look for a means of escape. Food can act as a tranquilliser:

> "… each time a person eats, the brain stimulates some of the neurochemicals, the endorphins, which are natural pain-killers, relaxants and pleasure stimulators … they are a God-given part of our mechanism, and certain activities stimulate them, such as laughter, sexual excitement, eating and aerobic exercise … This tranquillized state is normal and healthy. But the compulsive overeater may have become dependent on her own endorphins and the state of food-induced pleasure".[5]

Sam recalls the worst experience she had when feeling compelled to turn to food as an instant relief from pain. 'I found myself raiding the freezer in order to eat a whole chocolate sponge whilst having my first miscarriage. I was so terrified of what was happening to my body and of the unknown that, though ordered to stay on complete bed-rest, I crawled downstairs on my knees and ate my calmer whilst lying on the kitchen floor'.

## Burying anger
Depression and a sense of loss are often significant with compulsive eaters. Underneath depression there is

usually much repressed anger. Compulsive eating can be a 'safe way' to express forbidden anger – pushing down food is a means of pushing down feelings. 'The act of overeating provides active, physical release from pent-up anger while allowing the individual to be "nice" and avoid conflict'.[6]

The doctors at the Minirth-Meier Clinic in Dallas, Texas, make the observation that many of their patients are angry with themselves for something they have done, such as going too far sexually, and that they carry a load of guilt. They punish themselves by overeating then hate themselves for being overweight, which is often less painful than getting in touch with the anger they really feel for the wrong they have done.[7] Pushing anger down with food might solve the sufferer's problems for a while but the difficulty is that if every time she feels angry she chooses to react in this way, she never actually learns how to express and handle her anger. The anger does not just sit inside her and disintegrate over time – it stores up, anger upon anger, waiting to explode. Holding on to resentment results in a depletion of certain brain chemicals which causes loss of energy and motivation. If the person continues to eat at the normal rate, whilst being less active, she will gain weight.

A compulsive eater in flight from her anger does not usually realise that she is angry. Hand in hand with bingeing, she may push her anger towards others in a way which produces anger in them, at the same time proving that she is helpless, unable to cope or out of control. By doing this she hides it from herself. She need not deal with her fears about what her anger will do to others or how they might react. Instead she often feels the victim of others' exasperation. As a result she never has a chance to deal with the real issues underlying her anger and it is like a boomerang, turned back upon herself.[8]

The compulsive eater's weight is also sometimes used by her as a form of protection to keep other people's anger out. I remember when I was about nine we used to have a saying at my school: 'I am rubber, you are glue, everything nasty bounces off me and sticks on you!' The compulsive eater can be conveying a much more subtle version of the same saying.

If the sufferer does not like herself, which is usually the case, her fat can be seen as the place where all the disliked parts of her are stored. Everything which is unacceptable about herself, or life, may be blamed on the fact that she is fat. 'Some women who are very overweight unconsciously protect their self-image by disowning the fat, as if they were saying: "This is not me – I am the thin person within who has little to do with this enormous figure looking at me from the mirror"'.[9] If she is rejected or hurt by other people it is easier to feel that it's her fat which is being rejected not her.

Compulsive eaters may 'feel safer using their mouths to feed themselves than using them to talk and be assertive. They imagine that their fat is making the statement for them while the suffering prevents the words from coming out'.[10] Their weight can become their voice – a way of making quite strong statements about things'; a way of saying 'No', 'I need', 'I want', 'I hate', etc. In self-help groups I have heard compulsive eaters say that losing weight is like losing their voice.

## Hiding fear

Sometimes the compulsive eater eats to rebel against the 'perfect image'. She is fed up with trying to live up to the standards which are set. She may feel that she will never attain the 'perfect image' and so she goes to the other extreme of not only abstaining from competing but giving up caring about her body altogether.

Although they may give the impression of not being bothered about weight or, alternatively, always trying to lose weight, some compulsive eaters are afraid of being slim. Their fear is sometimes associated with having come to the conclusion that there are certain criteria which go with slimness. Despite hungering after these criteria, they are concerned that they won't achieve them. I asked several sufferers to write down what attaining slimness means. Some of these were being:

- in control
- happier
- sophisticated
- successful
- respected
- liked
- sexually attractive
- feminine
- wanted

Many compulsive eaters reason that it's easier not to compete in these things than to risk failing. They are not always conscious of choosing to opt out. They may not be aware of needing their fat until they lose it and experience slimness without having worked through the underlying issues, or are asked by a therapist to visualise what being slim feels like. The conclusions can be that being fat feels safer and enables them to cope with life. It also gives them a feeling of strength, compensating for lack of self-worth or confidence. Being slim or, even more so, thin means taking the risk of feeling vulnerable and raw, even cold. The compulsive eater 'is exposed to the very things she attempted to get away from when she got fat in the first place:[11]

> "Rea did not see herself in the same light as did her parents. She felt inadequate. She felt that she was a selfish, ungrateful and bad person … that she could not cope with her parents' demands and that she would be increasingly incompetent. Her fat expressed both the resentment at having to be so perfect and the

need to hide and contain the bad person she felt she was inside. She feared being thin because she felt she would then be everything her parents wanted; she would be in their image and without a self".[12]

If the very overweight sufferer were to lose weight she might also fear being unnoticeable. Her size causes people to pay attention to her, to hold doors open and to consider her needs. If she were to shrink physically she might disappear from people's view. The thought of being 'a nobody' is painful.

## Filling emptiness

The compulsive eater who feels empty inside may gain weight in order to feel more protected. Being physically empty can feel terrible because it means that she is likely to get in touch with her deep sense of emotional emptiness. Emptiness feels like death. It is as though emptiness is sitting there waiting to suck her into its dark vacuum and she will never experience the light of day again. For the sufferer who struggles against being emotionally close to other people but underneath longs for closeness, the emptiness is experienced as 'something missing' in her friendships. Food fills the gap which eases the pain and stops her from focusing too much on the unbearable void.

Often there is also a deep sense of loneliness which other people fail to recognise because the compulsive eater is usually someone who appears to be very involved with people and great fun. The loneliness is not so much through lack of the company of other people, but lack of relating with like-minded people – people who understand her. Loneliness can be an intensely painful encounter, along with a deep yearning and a sense of restlessness. Fear floods the personality bringing panic that there is nothing able to relieve the terrible ache. Food can easily become a companion at these times.

Many compulsive eaters began eating for comfort or to

dispel loneliness as children and have struggled with being overweight since childhood. Overweight children are frequently left out or they win approval by being the joker and funny. 'She's a good laugh' the other kids might say, but inside the child is feeling isolated or different. As an adult, the more the sufferer is able to allow others to get close the less she experiences the ache of loneliness, but mentally she often pushes other people away from her, protecting her raw inner self. In maintaining superficial relating she does not discover meaningful friendships. Feelings of rejection build up and the more she believes there is a perfect solution to it all the more disappointed she is, and the greater her sense of isolation. Erica started using food as a comfort when she was about twelve:

"At family gatherings my sister would be the sensible mature child (the role which I wanted to play), conversing with and accepted by the grown-ups. I would be the young, silly child who pulled funny faces and made people laugh. After I had made them laugh, I would go away and eat – partly to stop myself talking too much, partly to punish myself for being so unlikeable and partly to comfort myself and ease my inner conflict. This continued for many years without my acknowledging it or my unhappiness. I thought that this was what life was all about – an unhappy struggle. I hated school and didn't work. – my sister worked hard and loved it! Nobody knew how unhappy the lively, funny younger sister was and I didn't realise I could be happy".

The compulsive eater is generally someone who takes on a lot and keeps busy. Her inability to say 'No' is both a help and a hindrance to her. It prevents her from thinking too much about how she feels but it also stops her from protecting and looking after herself, which can still leave her feeling empty and lonely:

A trap has been hidden
  along my pathway.
Even if you look,
  you won't see anyone
who cares enough
  to walk beside me.
There is no place to hide,
  and no one who really cares.

I pray to you, Lord!
  'You are my place of safety,
and you are my choice
  in the land of the living'.
Please answer my prayer.
  I am completely helpless.
Psalm 142:3-6 CEV

# PART 2
## *THE UNFATHOMED DEPTHS*

# 5 | BACKGROUND: FAMILY AND EFFECTS

The family background is a very sensitive area. Often parents have been blamed for their child's eating disorder and carry much guilt. No one should blame the parents; they are the product of their own upbringing.

It would be helpful if the sufferer and her family read this chapter and express their thoughts and feelings to each other. What I am about to share is not easy reading, but for recovery to be possible all family members need to be honest about the way they relate, and to think carefully whether, for them, there is some truth in some of these words.

First, let's look at some of the qualities which constitute a well-balanced family. These include:

## Family members

- being open and honest in communication
- allowing anger and sadness to be an acceptable part of conversation and expressed appropriately
- feeling safe to disagree without fear of criticism, rejection or isolation
- being able to confess failure, along with acceptance of confession
- loving one another despite failure
- being unafraid to call 'badness' badness
- affirming each other's value and worth at every age
- being emotionally warm and gentle when hurt feelings are expressed
- being allowed to state their own opinions

- helping each other to discover and use their unique gifts

## Parents

- offering assurance that the children are loved no matter what they say or do
- allowing children age-appropriate choices
- creating an atmosphere where negative feelings and behaviour can be talked about and helped
- encouraging children to think for themselves
- showing the importance of vulnerability by expressing their own, and asking about other members' feelings
- being consistent in behaviour and promises, creating a predictably safe environment not a chaotic or confusing one
- setting limits which if not kept have consequences, without instilling guilt or fear
- understanding the reason for conflict before punishing
- willing to own their imperfections
- helping to make failures a means of learning, not condemnation[1]

Usually, the parents of sufferers are very caring people who genuinely want the best for their children but who sadly – due perhaps to their own needs not having been met in childhood, or hurts not having been worked through – have developed patterns of behaviour which can contribute to a family member developing an eating disorder. They provide well for their children in terms of physical, material and educational needs. Anorexic families are generally made up of high-achievers who are devoted, work hard and who show much self-control. The emphasis on self-control could be part of the reason for the child developing anorexia as opposed to the other eating disorders. Food and weight have often been significant in all eating disorder families. A high percentage of compulsive eaters have an overweight mother. Many anorexics and bulimics have a parent who is very weight or health conscious.

The father of a sufferer is described as emotionally uninvolved; rigid; distant; ambitious; a perfectionist; having high expectations of his children; uncomfortable with his and other people's feelings; non-assertive with his wife. A number of fathers have admitted to feeling 'second rate' or 'left out'. The mother is said to be anxious; controlling; negative; preoccupied with the physical well-being/safety of her children; having difficulty in seeing herself as a separate person; over-anxious to fulfil her children's need. It is also suggested that mothers 'are submissive to their husbands in many details and yet do not truly respect them'.[2]

## Blocked communication

Communication is one of the weaker aspects of the family. This may have developed out of the parents' own low self-esteem and instability. It is not unusual for marital relationships to be poor and for the child to form an alliance with one or both parents in a desperate attempt to 'help' the marriage. As a result, emotionally, the child may take on responsibilities which should not be hers, and feel very burdened. If the parents struggle to express love to one another openly, the child can sense that she is living in a 'loveless' environment and imagine that she is not loved.

Researchers who were sent into anorexic families reported that they felt uncomfortable when the whole family was together; they had to be careful not to 'make waves'; many of the parents were like needy children; the basic emptiness in the family and the parents' relationship showed up; the fathers had somewhat different upbringings from the mothers, which formed a vital part in the way the parents reacted to each other and their children.[3]

A study of bulimics indicated that the relationship with their parents was very poor. The sufferers felt that they were shown little attention; their parents did not spend much time with them and did not know them well; their parents tended to be reserved and unemotional; there was little affection expressed in the family. They would have liked to have communicated more with their parents and felt they did not have very meaningful conversations with their mother. A number said that they had not spent much time with their fathers as teenagers.[4]

The way the family members relate clearly has an effect on the children, and so it may seem strange if only one of those children develops an eating disorder. But even within the same family parents can relate differently to each child. Each child also has his/her own personality, depth of sensitivity, ways and means of coping. It is suggested that pre-anorexic children, unlike their siblings, are unable to cover up or control their childish behaviour. The siblings seem to escape getting involved in the patterns by withdrawing from family life or by seeming to be more as the parents want them to be. Pre-anorexic children come across as needing their parents more, and being very aware of the conflicts and neglects. They are vulnerable, compliant and take criticism and 'put downs' very seriously. The siblings may *appear* to survive better, but at a high price. They only avoid anorexia because they are involved in other obsessions, and it is likely they will hit problems elsewhere.[5]

Prior to the anorexia, the child has been seen as good, obedient and loveable, with few problems. Yet it is not uncommon for her to be feeling intense inner anguish. Childhood is experienced as very stressful and confusing. The child tends to feel that she is not good enough in that she does not live up to 'expectations' or that she could be in danger of losing her parents' love and consideration. But she conceals her discontent, behaving as if she were happy. She feels 'undeserving', 'unworthy' and 'ungrateful'. She often complains that she has received too many privileges and she feels burdened by having to live up to such 'specialness'.[6]

## Hidden shame

The type of family from which sufferers come is some-times described as shame-based. Shame is a feeling of being defective as a person. Maxine West, a psychologist, points out that in these families it is extremely important that members look and act appropriately. Many 'rules' exist to avoid situations which may tap into the shame of the parents. A 'front' is created and outsiders see and interact with this 'front', not with what is *really* happening in the family. This can affect the child's sense of reality. Control is imperative to survival.[7]

The only time you can be sure that an unspoken rule exists is if you break it. In such families, value and accept-ance are based on performance and members are afraid of what the existence of a problem 'says' about them.[8] The members are very keen to be especially nice to each other but in so doing often fail to speak directly, sometimes choosing to speak through another member. This style of relating takes a vast amount of energy and results in constantly striving to please other people, and feeling guilty when failing to do so.

Another aspect of the shame-based family is that the children may be expected to be adults. This is shown by childish behaviour being seen by the parents as 'bad' or 'messy' or 'out of control'. The parents' need to feel in control is very important. The child may have been prevented from experimenting in certain ways, such as with cooking, because one of the parents found coping with 'the mess' too uncomfortable.

## Unclear boundaries

Each family has its own set of boundaries and out of these a child begins to learn who she is as an individual and where she stands in relation to family members and outsiders. Marilyn Lawrence and Mira Dana indicate two extremes which can occur. In one type of family, privacy and being an individual are highly prized and it may be difficult for the members to feel close to each other, to share, or truly to relate. In another type of family the need for privacy is experienced as rejection. It is considered that everything should be shared; everyone has to know all about everyone else. Even feelings are family property; it can be impossible for one member to be upset without affecting the whole family.[9]

In the eating disorder family boundary problems mainly seem to exist between mother and daughter. Rebekah, who developed anorexia when she was four-teen, wrote ten years later as she was recovering:

"I have always been very close to my mother but I realise now that it has been an unbreathable closeness, where I feel that I am somehow expected to be a *part* of her, or she of me. She always has to know what I am doing and to be involved in my life, otherwise she feels left out. When I was a child she used to read my diary and I can remember thinking nothing's private. Sometimes it felt like I was being interrogated, just by her wanting to know things".

The greatest violation of boundaries is sexual abuse, where the doors of privacy are smashed open and the child's body is no longer experienced as her own. Other areas where boundaries may be crossed are breaking confidences; discounting opinions, feelings, and ideas; not respecting people's desires; not asking people's permission to use their belongings; reading other people's diaries and letters; talking about marital sexual matters in front of a child; emotionally leaning on a child, etc. Whatever the violation, it is going to erode a person's self-respect and trust of others and create a sense of lack of control. 'It is never the child's job to be there for the parent. It is the parent's job to be there for the child'.[10]

## Over-involvement

The potential for problems can begin long before anorexia. Donald Winnicott suggests that in the early stages in life a mother can anticipate her child's needs but if she continues to do so the child will not learn that her behaviour brings her the response she wants. A baby needs to discover that by crying she can 'tell' her mother that she is hungry. If the baby is never allowed to express her need, she may be well-nourished but she will not have learned that she has a voice to which people will respond.[11]

Many anorexics who have spoken to me come across as people who struggle in voicing their opinions, or in believing that others *want* to hear them; they passively wait for people to 'invite' them to participate. Their mothers seem to know their needs better than they do, and tend to 'speak for them'. The mothers also talk in terms of 'we' when speaking of their, or their daughter's needs/struggles. The family members frequently over-react to the choices which other members make. The results of these patterns are that what the potential anorexic fails to do is to develop a sense of her own worth as an independent person who is able to take control of her own life'.[12] She faces childhood lacking confidence in making her own decisions. As an adult she then finds coping with life by herself very difficult.
Maybe

> "... mothers try to stop their daughters from leading the kind of frozen and distraught lives they themselves led. In trying to 'save' their daughters they contribute heavily towards the development of anorexia. If such mothers could see this and try to help themselves by accepting their own rebellion and struggle, things would be a lot easier".[13]

The kind of relationship which often exists between the mother and adult daughter is more like that which exists between a mother and a much younger child. The daughter appears to believe that she depends for her very survival upon her mother, and the mother backs this up by her own behaviour. The mother might tell her daughter that she should take more responsibility for herself but her own behaviour belies her words.[14]

The mother could be fairly accurate in understanding her adult daughter's needs but stating these when her daughter is an adult is not appropriate. Natalie, who had been in an accident as a child and as a result was partially sighted, told me of an incident with her mother which illustrates this point. 'I took my mother to a meeting I attend every week. We sat where I often sit. Part way through she whispered, "There are some spare seats nearer the front. Perhaps we should move; it might be easier for you to see". Didn't she think, at thirty-two, I had the ability to know my own needs, and make choices?' When Natalie and her mother discussed this later, her mother explained that she was only trying to think of Natalie. Her mother's action had come out of kindness but what she had failed to realise was that, since they were on Natalie's territory and Natalie was an adult, perceiving Natalie's need took all responsibility away from her as a person able to make her own decisions. Her mother began to see Natalie's point and communication became the bridge to understanding and healing.

Salvador Minuchin has found anorexic families to be over-involved, over-protective, not willing to change, and tending to avoid conflict.[15] Palazolli indicates that the child, rather than the conflict between the parents, becomes the family problem. This focus on the child's symptoms serves to *express* as well as *avoid* the unresolved conflicts existing between the parents.[16] Conflict, in the anorexic home, can be sensed more in atmosphere than in words. If conflict is not *openly* expressed the child never learns how to resolve it, and will remain frightened of situations where even differing opinions are spoken. The anorexic's goals become approval and love rather than knowledge or competence. She will develop an obsessional concern for perfection, resulting in low self-esteem. She will also struggle with extreme self-consciousness, making it difficult for her to form relationships outside the family and creating increased dependency upon the approval of her parents.[17]

It is reported that despite the children of compulsive eating families being intelligent, they cling to their mothers. Their mothers still do things for them, way after the children are capable of doing things for themselves. Mothers also compensate for insecurity by excessive feeding, so food has an exaggerated emotional meaning and can be a substitute for love, security and satisfaction. The mothers see muscular activity and social contacts as being associated with danger and separation, which can have the effect of the child failing to adjust well socially or being emotionally immature. As an adolescent the sufferer often thought that her father's interest was only in how well she looked or how successful she was, and not in what she valued or how she felt.[18]

## Suppressed feelings

In her late teens Leigh became bulimic. For much of her childhood her mother was an alcoholic and her father absorbed in his work. As she spoke of her family background, she described aspects of family life which are fairly typical for many bulimics:

> "I guess things were pretty chaotic. As a family we didn't really communicate and certainly didn't trust each other. The 'rules' which existed were inconsistent and my parents didn't seem to be there for me emotionally. As far as feelings were concerned, negative ones were *not* good news, and it's almost like my feelings weren't a part of me. I somehow had to get rid of the feelings of which my parents didn't approve,

otherwise I couldn't feel accepted. As a child I believed that whatever my parents said, or implied, was right so when negative feelings were frowned on I believed that I must be 'bad for having them. Sometimes I still feel like that".

Having to keep negative feelings underground, along with the father's obvious discomfort with expression of feelings, teaches the child that she must suppress how she *really* feels in order to be 'acceptable'. The eating disorder family finds it hard to cope with certain feelings, such as anger, and the members are not encouraged to discuss how they feel. The parents often consider that feelings need to be understood, or exist for a good reason, and somehow don't expect their children to be upset. They may discount their children's feelings by stating that whatever has happened can't be that bad, or quell their emotions by inferring that children shouldn't feel that way. The trouble is that when children shut down the painful emotional side they also lose the ability to express the joyous side. If parents are unable to meet their own needs, they will struggle to meet the needs of their children. Instead, without realising, they create an atmosphere which prevents the healthy expression of feelings:

"Members aren't allowed to question the family rules or to voice thoughts or feelings that conflict with these rules. Disagreement is met with rejection. Children from this type of home don't learn to communicate openly and directly. They don't learn that one can disagree with someone else and still have the person's respect and acceptance … they become afraid to express themselves, until eventually they don't have a clue as to who they are or how they feel. They learn to avoid conflict at any price, to swallow 'unacceptable' thoughts and feelings so as not to upset others, and constantly to fear rejection".[19]

The children can come away with the sense that they are not loved and accepted, or if they are, it is only if, or when, they perform. They can feel that they are not valuable or worthwhile. They often feel very alone and as though they do not really belong anywhere.[20]

The child who goes on to develop an eating disorder can easily fear that if she expresses negative feelings or she displeases her parents she will be rejected. She becomes 'prickly' with her parents and, as they attempt to get close to her, it is as though they are touching a live wire.

The problems which have been talked about in this chapter do not necessarily stop when a child leaves home – these can equally well take place between a parent and adult child as they can between a parent and child. If the patterns are not fully dealt with the sufferer may also carry unhealthy ways of relating into other relationship, including raising her own family.

# 6 | SEXUALITY: ATTITUDES AND ABUSE

Whatever the eating disorder there is an element of being unsure about how to handle sexuality, and food and weight are used as a means of expressing the confusion.

## Fear of growing up

Anorexia is sometimes associated with a fear of growing up and sexual maturity. The pre-anorexic child is said to be behind her peers in terms of emotional and sexual adjustment, and it is not uncommon for her to feel ashamed of the bodily changes taking place at puberty. The idea of getting rid of the signs of sexual development, such as fat around the hips; and putting an end to menstruation, which is a monthly reminder of adult responsibility and leaves her feeling dirty, can be appealing. She may think that others will expect her to be 'different' now that she has started to menstruate, or she may feel not yet ready to change. Some anorexics also link menstruation and the ability to have intercourse; on starting their periods, the thought that *they* can now 'do this' disgusts them. Such extreme thinking is usually found in an anorexic who is young, has not dated, and does not binge and vomit at all. As she gets older it is likely that such thinking will decrease. If she begins to put on weight, but has not worked through her sexuality struggles, she may choose to wear clothes which make her look 'hipless' or flatchested, showing that she would still rather stay a child than become sexual. Even the anorexic who marries is often wanting childlike comfort, more than sexual contact.

The anorexic puts off facing her womanhood. She closes her eyes to her fears half believing that sexuality will 'go away'. Jasmine, a fifteen-year-old who frequently used to write to me, said, 'I do want to grow up, but I don't want to be like a woman'. Male sufferers struggle in a similar way. Richard, looking back on his experience, said, 'I was very immature and wasn't really aware of sex or girls until my twenties. Sex was never spoken about in our home and was not considered a "nice" part of life. I felt my sexuality was too fragile to show and, through dieting, I began to shut down any sexual feelings'.

The process of developing sexually is easier to cope with if the young person is given information about how her body changes, and is able to talk to someone about her fears and guilt. Most sufferers recall not having had anyone they could talk to at the vital time, or not even realising that talking about it was an option. It is easy for the sufferer to feel that her friends speak with great confi dence about growing up, which only accentuates her own struggles. If she did not see her parents demonstrate affec- tion to each other on a regular basis she will not have learnt how to relate to the opposite sex. Also, if she does not have many friends, is shy, or lonely, the thought of now being expected to have a boyfriend, when she is already feeling insecure, could be enough to make her want to escape physical maturity.

Puberty scares a sufferer because changes are happening to her over which she has no control. These changes are often taking place at the same time as the need for control becomes all important in her life. Her fear drives her to take a drastic measure such as starvation.

Anorexics and bulimics are very critical of their bodies. At puberty they may examine their changing shape and, in shock, think 'Help! I'm fat. I must get rid of it'. They see this as the need to be slim rather than as a struggle in connection with their sexuality.

In the minds of bulimics, bulimia and sexual activity

are closely linked; they may use intercourse or masturbation as a means of thwarting a bulimic attack, or bingeing to the point of sedation to lessen their sexual feelings.[1] Leigh said that, for her, bulimia uses the same energy as sex. 'But bulimia is safer – there isn't the risk of someone hurting you; you're not made vulnerable'. Some bulimics, describing how their eating is out of control, say that they also fear becoming promiscuous. There is a hunger for love which is sometimes mistakenly thought of as a hunger for sex. But there is often a lack of contentment in sex because it is not satisfying her true need. A number of married bulimics have said that they are more interested in being cuddled and held than in having sexual intercourse.

Like bulimics, compulsive eaters may sometimes use food to satisfy their sexual needs. Being fat also stops a person from having to compete to be sexually attractive. In one group it was seen as providing sexual protection. Fat prevents them from considering themselves as sexual.[2] To be slim can mean that the compulsive eater's sexuality is too exposed, which may feel very uncomfortable. 'She imagines that if she loses the weight she will be losing a protective coating against the world'.[3]

## Parents' own struggles

The way each parent feels about his or her sexuality and behaves towards each other and their developing child will mould the child's attitude. Problems can arise if parents:

- are unable to relate sexually
- have a negative attitude towards the opposite sex
- are anxious about their own bodies
- do not allow children privacy
- frequently expose their own nakedness
- are involved in extra-marital affairs
- give the children too much or too little information on sexual development

- deny sexual feelings
- tease the children in their development
- are negative in the children's interest in dating
- state that they would have preferred to have had a child of the opposite sex

When the mother is unquestionably in touch with her own femininity she gives to her daughter a love of being a woman and a basic faith in life. When the mother is negative the daughter is hampered in making emotional adjustments and fails to take the natural steps towards feminine maturity. Only if the girl has been allowed to live her own life, has learned to value herself and her feelings, will she be able to cope with reality in a creative way. What the mother passed on to the girl, and the father's respect for the mother as a feminine being, are crucial to natural maturing.[4]

## Sexual abuse

A fairly high percentage of victims of sexual abuse go on to develop an eating disorder. Many people fail to realise the connection, or do not class their experience as abuse, because it did not involve intercourse; was followed by the abuser being kind; or caused sexual arousal and so, in part, was pleasurable. Whatever the extent of the abuse it is going to cause problems in a person's life. Abusive situations could include:

- a child's privacy not being respected
- questioning a child as to why she does not like a parent's nakedness
- an adult exposing himself
- sexually abusive words
- pornography
- a parent taking an excessive interest in a child's development or a teenager's dating experience
- masturbation in front of a child

- asking a child to touch or wash a parent around the genitals
- fondling
- inappropriate kissing
- oral sex
- intercourse

The abuser can be a family member or an outsider. In some situations the abuse is so painful that the child blocks it out altogether. Shelley was raped by a stranger when she was twelve years old. As a young adult she became a compulsive eater:

> "Since a teenager I have had bouts of depression. After I'd had counselling and talked about the rape I thought I could get on with my life. Instead I went deeper and deeper into depression. I started to get nightmares and flashbacks of my father sexually abusing me. I became a wreck, not knowing what to do. I was full of self-hatred. The overeating died down but instead I started to drink and harm myself by cutting my arms and taking overdoses. Slowly I saw this was not the way to live. I had to start dealing with the problems".

The home of an abused child can set her up for abuse. There is often distance in relating. Two of the factors which are essential to a happy home would have been absent: the sense of being enjoyed for who she is rather than for what she does, and the opportunity to develop separateness from the other members of the family. The child might have carried adult burdens; have been led to believe that certain feelings are wrong, crazy, or non-existent. The atmosphere in the home might have been demanding, conservative, or rule bound; the highest value being loyalty to protect the family. The child would, to some extent, have felt empty, committed to pleasing people, and would not have had clear boundaries.[5]

Feeling hungry for emotional attention the child may take whatever is offered. When she becomes a victim of abuse she feels that the abuse is her fault. The conviction that she is bad begins to grow, destroying her self-esteem and her ability to relate to, or feel accepted by, others. Because the damage is not being dealt with, as an adult she will inevitably develop unhealthy patterns such as eating disorders, self-harm, promiscuity, withdrawal, or aggression. In most cases the abuse survivor dare not talk about her experience for fear of offending those close to her, digging up unbearable pain or facing the fact that she feels like two different people.

It is not uncommon for the survivor to find herself under a psychiatrist, a very hurting and confused person, classed as mentally unstable, yet with her real pain not having been addressed. Mandy explains her experience:

"I had an incestuous relationship with my brother in my teens. I felt intensely guilty and terrified that I was pregnant. I am sure that this was the final straw which sent me into anorexia – a desperate bid to reverse the risk of pregnancy and the experiences associated with a maturing physical body. It was only during my third hospital admission that I had the courage to tell someone. I was then told by a nurse that I'd had experiences similar to a lot of other people, but they didn't react like me so what was all the fuss about? I was devastated and kept my feelings to myself for another five years".

## Crippling effects

The effects of sexual abuse are many. The person can feel guilty, dirty, rejected, disgusted and different. The survivor often believes that it was her own desire to be cared for, wanted, hugged and loved which led to the abuse. She 'feels deceived by her body; the body is the enemy, and were it not for the body there would never have been a problem'.[6] The most powerful emotions which are carried around are shame, anger, and powerlessness. Shame, because the whole experience has left the person feeling defective. Instead of realising that the abuser has done something wrong the child believes that she deserves to be hurt. The anger may be directed at people in general because she feels betrayed rather than protected. More often, though, it is directed towards herself for being such a 'wicked' person who didn't do anything to stop the abuse. The anger is rarely recognised, but rather comes out in the way the survivor reacts towards others, puts herself down, or hurts herself. She felt powerless as a child and continues to do so as an adult. She believes that she does not have choices and that she cannot change her circumstances. She doesn't value herself enough to choose to walk away from situations where people treat her badly, and as a result she is easily hurt again. It feels as though she wears a label on her head saying, 'Come and abuse me'. Sometimes she considers that it's easier to accept punishment than love.

Bulimics who have been abused can feel a great sense of relief in vomiting, and live in the hope that the 'vile thing inside' might be vomited up. As a child Anita had been forced to have oral sex with her father:

> "I have always felt that my father was inside me. I couldn't explain it, but I couldn't get him out. The vomiting was my bid to get rid of that part of him. The fear was of not getting rid of what had gone into me. I feel weak and bad when I eat and maybe that has something to do with a feeling that my throat and my whole inner part is contaminated and violated".

Bridget had been sexually assaulted as a teenager and has consequently suffered with anorexia for over fifteen years.

She is terrified of returning to the weight she was when the assault took place in case her feelings in connection with the assault return. The anorexic whose weight creeps up can feel horrified at having a sexually mature and receptive body when her emotions are still stuck at the age at which she had been abused.

Survivors of satanic ritual abuse have the added problems of eating reminding them of some of the foul and inhumane things they were forced to eat and do as children. Marcia had often been deprived of food as a child, and later developed anorexia. 'My hunger made me vulnerable to the cult's power and their demands. I equated my hunger with weakness and powerlessness'.[7]

When faced with the memories of any kind of abuse, people turn to all sorts of drastic measures and find themselves doing things of which they feel ashamed. They may fantasise about certain aspects of the abuse; change the circumstances; speak as though it is still happening; talk in a child's voice; dissociate (go somewhere else whilst their body remains in the same place, separating body from feelings); or develop many personalities. All are means of trying to cope with the horror.

## Why eating disorders?

Most people do not want to face the abuse, and eating disorders can seem to help a person cope in various ways with the painful effects.

**1. By being a form of protection**. For the abuse survivor there is often a desire for protection from further hurt or exposure; a fear of intimacy; an inability to trust; a feeling of not belonging. By becoming obsessed with food – what to eat and what not to eat – and by forming a relationship with food where it, rather than people, brings comfort, the survivor has a greater chance of protecting herself from being wounded by others. For the anorexic and the compulsive eater, changing her body to being unattractive to the opposite sex also limits her chance of being involved in an unwanted sexual relationship.

**2. By dealing with the horror of feelings**. The pain of sexual abuse feels unbearable and in order to survive the child has to shut down her emotions. Rage, guilt and shame must be deadened. Self-harm often becomes the only way the survivor knows how to express the horrendous pain when it does emerge. Cutting or burning herself releases pent-up energy and is a means of making visible what is going on inside her. Another way of coping with the feelings is through overdoses, which are intended to 'kill' the feelings without necessarily killing the person. A survivor may take an overdose in an attempt to 'have a rest' from the conflicts inside, or to express the desire to be protected.

**3. By taking the focus away from the real problem**. If the survivor develops an eating disorder both she and other people will believe that the eating disorder is her problem, which will keep the attention away from the abuse. Also, so long as she concentrates on her eating and weight she will not have time to think about how devastating the abuse was. Unless the person helping her has knowledge of the connection between sexual abuse and eating disorders, the sexual abuse may remain undealt with, and she will have escaped confronting a large part of the cause.

**4. By attempting to neutralise the feeling of being dirty**. For some people the eating disorder, with its accompanying rituals such as compulsive hand-washing, extreme tidiness, cleanliness and orderliness, can be a means of trying to eradicate the dirt left by the abuse.

**5. By creating a feeling of control**. Wanting never to feel powerless again, the survivor takes control of her life. Some anorexics admit that having anorexia makes them feel special and admired by others, which helps them to feel less worthless as a result of the abuse. The anorexic needs to take control of her body to try to get rid of the terrible flaw she feels exists. The bulimic and compulsive eater experience lack of control in order to reassert control over the body. 'It is deeply comforting to these patients to emerge from a binge and regain stringent control over their bodies and behaviour, partly because this demonstrates their personal power over their body, and partly because it is a displacement of responsibility'.[8] In taking control of her appetite for food the sufferer can feel that she is also taking control of her sexual appetite.

Whilst developing an eating disorder appears to help the survivor, in the end it brings greater pain. Pushing other people away in order to protect herself isolates her, sets her up for crippling loneliness, and reinforces the feeling that she is different and not acceptable. What remains is a terrible inner ache; a silent scream. If she can't acknowledge what is causing the torment, she will not experience anyone listening, which forces her to feel even more alone.

# 7 | HUNGER: INSIDE AND OUT

The sufferer's hunger for, or rejection of, food is not so much physical, but emotional. The anorexic who declares that she is not hungry and denies her needs is also someone who is afraid that once she starts eating, or admitting to her needs, she won't be able to stop. The bulimic and compulsive eater can also relate to this insatiable appetite.

Everyone has needs which they long to have met, but when the neediness is intense this usually stems from having been deprived in some way as a child. Children require meaningful time and attention from their parents that is not interrupted by the parents' needs, does not demand back, and is not filled with anxiety. If needs are not met, or they are seen as bad, weak, childish or selfish, then the person can be left with an empty void.

For the anorexic, who can't face the fact that she is still emotionally hungry, it becomes easier to pretend that she isn't hungry, physically or emotionally. She feels ashamed of having needs. Whilst it's all right for others to have them, she must somehow be above such things. Needs are a sign of weakness and she wants to achieve self-sufficiency. Marilyn Lawrence and Mira Dana believe that what the anorexic sees reflected in the mirror is not just her body, but a symbolic part of herself. It is the needy, demanding, yearning part which she so desperately tries to kill by starving her body, but which screams out to her 'I want to be seen, noticed, listened to'. This may be the reason for her still seeing herself as enormous when really she is emaciated.[1] Looking back on her experience of anorexia Sheena realised that she could create a hunger and control its satisfaction by exercising and starving. 'But, ultimately I had no rest or peace; a continual war waged within me'.

Both the bulimic and the compulsive eater find it easier than the anorexic to admit to having needs, although the thought frightens them. The bulimic often feels her neediness, and then suddenly senses that she must push it away. She fears that people may not like her for it:

> "At one moment, she feels a sense of uncontrollable neediness ... She attempts to 'deal with' her emotional needs with food, and the violence and ferocity with which she eats gives us some indication of the strength of those needs and the desperation she feels to calm her disturbed feelings. As soon as she has eaten, the bulimic woman feels a compulsion to get rid of the food and to free herself of any reminder of her awful and terrifying needs".[2]

The compulsive eater

> "... very often feels needy and empty as though she desperately wants something inside her. However, instead of allowing herself to be fully aware of what those needs really are, she reaches for food and submerges her needs ... At the same time, she feels terribly guilty about her needs. She cannot perceive them and attempt to meet them in a straightforward way. Her needs are a source of shame, which is represented by her fat ..."[3]

The compulsive eater is so emotionally hungry that her concern is that no one or nothing will *ever* fill the hole. If she admits to her neediness it may mean experiencing disappointment and emptiness. When she diets it is sometimes a desperate attempt to kill the hunger inside. But as she diets she gets more in touch with the hunger and quickly returns to eating.

## Love and nurturing

The sufferer longs to be loved for who she is, as she is, and not for what she can do or for being compliant. There is a part of her which can find satisfaction only through unconditional love. Lack of unconditional love as a child goes on affecting a person for as long as the deprivation is not faced and dealt with. If the sufferer's parents were not accepting the love they needed from God, and were not giving love to one another, they may have looked to the child to meet their needs. The child's resources, owing to being so young, have not had time to fill up and will slowly be emptied, leaving her in a perpetual state of emotional hunger.

In order to *feel* loved, a child needs not only to hear loving words, but to receive tenderness. This need does not diminish as the child grows. A teenager who is not treated with gentleness can feel a terrible loss. Jasmine was struggling with guilt over coming from a 'loving' home, and yet not feeling loved. 'I know my family love me, but somehow it doesn't feel the right kind of love'. The longing for love is also a longing for safety, protection and intimacy. Intimacy, for many sufferers, can feel frightening because it requires vulnerability. 'In early childhood, being vulnerable usually resulted in feeling abandoned and alone'.[4]

Some people, as they begin to acknowledge their needs, feel like a child inside. Many believe that the level of caring for which they long is only appropriate for children. Rosie used to visit the Samaritans. On one occasion the Samaritan asked Rosie how she had felt as a child. 'Lonely, afraid, empty and full of pain. I longed to be held and to feel love and affection'. 'And what about now?', the Samaritan said. Rosie started to sob deeply. 'It's OK to have needs as an adult', the Samaritan replied. Rosie realised that her needs as an adult were the same as when she was a child. She had never really felt her hunger before because she had blocked it out through developing anorexia. Now, having given up the anorexia as her way of coping, she was facing her hunger inside. She acknowledged a desperate craving to be nurtured, and yet she hated the needy part of herself because it interfered with the image of her as someone who was capable and strong. Her needs felt like a bottomless pit. Inside she knew that she would never feel fully alive unless she faced her needs. She had to admit that she longed for the care of others, and at the same time realised that people could not always be there in the way she wanted.

When someone is in pain, food is a quick and easy form of being nurtured; a chocolate bar can sometimes feel as comforting as an arm round the shoulder. At least with a chocolate bar the person feels she can choose to have another if she wants, which is not always possible with love and nurturing. Doctors Donald Klein and Michael Liebowitz, following extensive research, discovered that when someone is in love their body produces a chemical called phenylethylamine. Chocolate is loaded with that very same substance.[5] People often turn to chocolate when in reality they would like to be secure in the arms of someone who cares for them. Eating may be a way to stop thinking about the need for other people; bingeing can be an intimate process.

If it isn't food that a person is really longing for though, food will never satisfy. Ultimately the sufferer is searching for love but, having been hurt, she puts up barriers in friendship. She builds a protective layer through which love cannot fully penetrate. Even when others reach out to her she feels alone and distant and does not understand why.

## Touch and hugging
An important aspect of love and nurturing is being

touched and hugged. Non-sexual touch can speak volumes. Penny, a woman who had been through rejection and abuse as a child, and years of anorexia and bulimia as an adult, tells of how she feels desperate for warmth and affection. 'I long to be held'. Hugging is soothing emotionally and physically. The problem is in finding the hugs. The isolation, particularly for people who live on their own, can be devastating. A person may not receive significant touch for weeks, even months. Others feel that once they receive or ask for a hug, while it may feel good, it only accentuates their usual sense of isolation. As a teenager Amber needed to be cuddled:

> "I didn't think I could ask anyone to cuddle me. I felt I had to make up a really good reason – some kind of big problem or loss so that the cuddle would be legitimate. I only wanted to be cuddled by women or girls – I supposed I wanted them to be like mothers. I used to day-dream about it, but if people actually did cuddle me I would feel disgusted with myself. A few days later I'd want to be cuddled again. When I was being cuddled I felt like I could hang onto that person; to be sure, for a short while, that someone valued me and wasn't judging me".

Hugging feels good; dispels loneliness; overcomes fears; opens doors to feelings; builds self-esteem; eases tension; and fights insomnia. But hugging costs. It requires a person to be vulnerable. The fee for hugging is the risk that our hugs will be rebuffed or misinterpreted. If, as a child, we were deprived of love and touch we become unwilling to pay the fee of vulnerability. Love held back can turn to pain. When we risk our hugs, we affirm our wonderful ability to share. If we reach out and touch others, we are free to discover compassion and the capacity for joy.[6]

Hugs also say a number of things: I understand how you feel; you are special; you are who you are, not just what you do; you can feel safe; you can trust me to be here and support you. Hugs offer belonging, strength and healing.[7] One girl longed for hugs so much that she used to keep a secret tally of how many times teachers at school hugged her. Another said, 'I often feel if God would just hug me everything would be better'.

## Self-worth and security

What we believe others think of us often rules how we feel about ourselves and how we act towards others. The conclusions we come to about ourselves are formed at a very early age. Negative experiences in life then act as confirmation. 'Significant adults, such as parents, older siblings and teachers become the "mirrors" in which young children see themselves'.[8] Sufferers talk about how much they dislike themselves. Many feel different from others. They can't cope with reality, or with people. They switch to another world – the world of fantasy. They long for a place where they can feel safe and secure because the real world seems such a jungle.

> "People with a good self-esteem are comfortable with themselves. They accept themselves, including their shortcomings. This acceptance doesn't stop them from making changes, it frees them to do so. They are able to have a balanced estimate of themselves. They can be fully in touch with their emotions, but not controlled by them".[9]

The positive influences a child needs in order to develop a good self-worth are:

- attention (listening, eye contact, touch)
- acceptance (not earned through conformity or performance)

- affirmation (praise not only for achievement but for qualities)
- affection (loving even when unable to love in return)

The extent to which a child experiences the reverse of these is the extent to which self-worth will be impaired.[10] A disruption in the natural love process that a child requires can take place through various means. Situations which sufferers have shared have been boarding school; hospitalisation; death of a parent; a parent being preoccupied with work; divorce; separation or extramarital affairs.

When people have a low self-worth they often suffer from depression. They see themselves negatively; life negatively (demanding and unfair); the future negatively (without hope).[11] Other long-term effects include stress; guilt; anger; jealousy; loneliness; intimacy; failure; and a distorted picture of God. People try to compensate for their poor self-worth through different means: excessive shyness; drawing attention to themselves; putting themselves down; boasting; always having to be right; suspicion and criticism; rigid thinking; aggression; overwork.[12]

The sufferer is also someone who finds it hard to accept compliments. In her eyes the person who compliments her must be stupid, because otherwise they could see plainly that she is an 'awful person'. She doesn't feel that she deserves to be cared for, believing that she is 'a nothing'. She can't understand why others would want to help her, and so may even be suspicious of their help.

The anorexic's body-size represents the way she feels about herself. She views herself as so small and insignificant that if she existed in a normal body she would rattle around. Not eating is both a visible way of explaining to the world that she is 'a nobody' and, at the same time, a desperate attempt to regain some worth through rigid self-control. Her worth as a child was often based on the opinions of other people and whether or not she pleased them. The need to please others in order to feel of worth becomes a way of life.

The bulimic sees herself as bad inside. Her self-worth is measured in terms of being in control of her eating. Her worth will go up and down depending on how 'good' she has been, and how she looks. For the compulsive eater who hates herself, stuffing herself with sweet foods that are not good for her is very easy. She may feel that she doesn't even deserve nice food, served on a plate, and eaten politely.

For many women, especially those who go on to develop an eating disorder, self-image (the way we see ourselves) centres around body-image (the picture we have of our bodies).[13] The sufferer needs to begin to look at herself in a wider light. Her body is only a small part of her. There are also intelligence; understanding; relating; inner qualities; beliefs; and personality. All contribute towards her being a *unique* individual.

## Acceptance and recognition

Everyone longs to feel accepted and understood; to have recognition and a sense of purpose in their lives. Penny continued to tell me: 'At the moment I feel so empty, lost and confused. I no longer have any clear aim in life and I don't know where I am heading. It comforts me to starve myself periodically – to know that I can still lose weight'.

People's attempts to meet their needs for success fall into two broad categories: compulsiveness and withdrawal. Some put extra effort into work and try to say just the right thing to please those around them. These people may have a compelling desire to be in control of every situation. They may use practically anything and anybody to meet their need. Other people resort to withdrawal. These people try to avoid failure and disapproval by avoiding risks. They gravitate towards those who are kind, keeping clear of relationships which might demand vulnerability, and consequently, the risk of rejection. They may appear to be easygoing, but inside they are usually running from every potential situation that might not succeed.[14]

The child's feelings of acceptance or rejection grow out of other people's messages, either spoken or unspoken. As a child Natalie was told over and over 'People aren't going to like you if you pull that face'. The face she was pulling was in response to inner pain. She was desperately sad and confused as a child. She soon learned that to feel unhappy was unacceptable. Since she was suffering from depression as a teenager she felt sure that she must be a 'terrible person' who was disliked by everyone.

When children are in an environment where they are constantly put down, at home or at school, they can easily feel that they don't belong. They grow into adults who find it hard to trust people, and are afraid of being abandoned. Most sufferers long to be valued as an individual, not just as a part of the family or peer group, Keeping people at a distance creates an intense feeling of loss of connection, which would otherwise partially meet the sufferer's need for acceptance and recognition. If the sufferer does not feel accepted, she may find it hard to accept others with their faults.

The sense of isolation and lack of acceptance is often described as a feeling of being 'different' or 'cut off'. I remember a painting I did whilst anorexic: the silhouette of a person split in two enclosed in a glass bubble; reaching out, but unable to touch the outside world. It was a picture of desperate hunger in a land of plenty. There is hope though. The sufferer does not have to be left haunted by her hunger, as we will see in the final chapters of the book.

# PART 3
## *THE JOURNEY THROUGH*

# 8 | DECISION TO CHANGE

'I'm paranoid with fear. I feel so helpless. I don't know how to cope', Pippa wrote in her diary. 'I do want to get well but *nobody* seems to understand'. On 10 January she wrote: 'My body is dying and I am scared stiff'. Her weight fluctuated a little and then dropped dramatically in the weeks that she was waiting to be admitted to an eating disorder unit. In October she died in Intensive Care.

Many people are pessimistic about recovery. Figures showing the percentage of people who recover vary. Both short-term and long-term studies of patients with anorexia indicate that full recovery occurs in fewer than 50 per cent of the patients studied.[1] Calculating the average outcome in nine representative studies it was shown that 22 per cent of patients with anorexia, most of whom had been hospitalised, remained chronically ill or had a poor outcome, 8 per cent died. These figures were derived from a follow-up averaging ten years.[2] Comparable studies have not yet been conducted for bulimia or compulsive eating, but poor outcome is also known to be common.

Before a sufferer can change she needs to look at the advantages and disadvantages of having an eating disorder. If there are still too many advantages then change will be impossible. Only she can decide when she is ready. Alissa started to see that her eating disorder was hindering her: 'I realised that I was in the jaws of a monster I had created; I had to recognise I had a problem. But what could I do about it? Basically I had three options:

to die; to stay the way I was; or to change. The first was out of the question. The second was unbearable. The only other alternative was to recover'.[3]

Recovery begins with the sufferer admitting that she has a problem and being honest with herself and at least one other person. 'Awareness and compulsion cannot possibly exist together in the same moment. When you turn on a light, it is no longer dark'.[4] The sufferer has to learn to trust herself. 'Trusting yourself means being willing to discover the truth about yourself. And to value the process of discovering that truth'.[5] Part of her discovering the truth is facing herself, her hurts and her defences.

As with recovery from any potentially serious illness it will take time, require patience and care. It is necessary for the sufferer to listen to her own body, to be kind to herself and to rest when rest is needed. Some days will feel good whilst others will feel terrible. She will need to be helped to feel in control without control being essential for her feelings of worth and security. Recovery is possible as control is no longer seen as the answer to her problems.

## Too afraid to let go

Getting better can be frightening. At first it can feel worse than being in the throes of an eating disorder, but this will pass. As a person faces her problems often she feels like two people – one who wants to be rid of the eating disorder and one who doesn't. It is natural to wonder how she will cope without it. It has been her protection; comfort; guard against feelings; barrier to sexuality; destroyer of loneliness; form of identity and, although sometimes her enemy, also her friend. She has carried it around with her all day, every day – what will she think about if she isn't constantly thinking of food and exercise programmes?

One of the hardest aspects of recovery for the anorexic is to accept weight gain. What if she can't stop eating and ends up looking like a hippo? Maintaining her weight means losing the sense of achievement which weight loss creates. This is a terrifying thought because it has been the focus of her life since she became ill. The black and white thinking of anorexics and bulimics causes them to believe that the options are either starvation or stuffing. They fail to realise that there is plenty of scope between the two. Compulsive eaters may fear that in being thin they will feel unprotected and not be noticed. 'Fears about food and eating can only be overcome when the sufferer changes the way she sees herself and develops an optimistic view of her prospects ... She cannot enjoy food until she can enjoy life'.[6]

To look at the end goal of full recovery usually sends a sufferer into panic. If she can begin to see that she is not expected to change overnight, and that there are stages in her recovery, she will find it far easier to cope. *She* is in control and *she* determines the speed of recovery, except where medical intervention is necessary to save life.

## Seeking help

The sufferer's attitude towards receiving help will be based partly on past experience. If she has had unpleasant handling or unsuccessful treatment she may be reluctant to try again. But it is never worth giving up looking for the right kind of help.

Even after finding a therapist to whom she can relate the sufferer can still have mixed feelings. She will discover that sometimes she believes that the therapist is on her side and at other times the therapist seems to be against her. At some stage she will relate to her therapist the way she relates to others. If she withdraws, creates situations where she wants to be rescued, or pushes other people away in friendships, she will repeat the same pattern in therapy. She will inevitably feel angry and frustrated with her therapist, who is encouraging her to confront her behaviour, make changes and no longer sabotage herself.

One of the most important aspects of helping herself is that she makes the decision to share her anger with the therapist in the therapy session. If she hides her feelings she is in danger of ending the therapy, claiming that it was 'no good' and moving on to the next person to repeat the same pattern.

Different defensive reactions are taken into therapy. The anorexic may not admit that she needs much help or she may accept only those parts of the help she wants. She may be afraid of offending the therapist or see receiving help as self-indulgence. Therapy to her can feel like a burden at times, with the therapist seen as yet another person setting standards and someone she has to avoid upsetting. The bulimic may feel she needs help and then push it away; that she needs help one week and not the next, or frequently she turns up late or cancels at the last minute. She may consider that the therapist, whom she initially thought had all the answers, isn't good enough. The compulsive eater may feel that she needs more help than she is getting and seek additional support on the side. She may think that her problem isn't being solved quickly enough, become dependent on the therapist, or feel that the therapist won't be able to cope with the extent of her needs.

## Family changes
Some of the interactions between the parents and sufferer will have been feeding the eating disorder. The decision to change involves the sufferer making adjustments to the way she sees her parents, and her parents altering the way they handle their daughter. When she becomes aware of her parents' shortcomings, and is irritated or hurt by negative attitudes, criticism or over-reaction, it is useful for her to bear in mind that these may come from her parents' own pain – past or present. Their history may affect the way they have responded to her, both before and during her eating disorder.

It is helpful if the sufferer and her family set boundaries together concerning talking over the eating disorder. This can enable family members not to experience the eating disorder taking over their lives and help the sufferer not to feel constantly invaded by probing questions. All members need to be honest with each other but also respect each other's wishes for privacy on certain matters. Honesty should always be for the *good* of the other person. 'Love without honesty is sentimentality, but honesty without love is brutality'.[7]

An important decision for the sufferer is not to demand, manipulate or expect others to read her mind, but to ask. Learning to express her feelings and knowing that she has a right to do so is a part of the recovery journey. In some situations she will need to choose to react in a different way from her usual one. For instance, if parents treat an adult sufferer as a child, instead of the sufferer giving in and burying resentment towards them, she must choose to respond as an adult. This then gives the parents the message that she no longer wishes to be treated as a child, and offers them permission to react to her as an adult next time. The sufferer can only take responsibility for *her* altered reactions. If the parents do not change that is not her responsibility.

It is essential that if the family is to help, rather than hinder, they understand about eating disorders. Reading books, talking with someone who is well informed, making contact with an eating disorder association or attending a self-help group are some of the best ways of being educated. Progress cannot easily be made whilst parents deny that there is a problem or consider that the problem belongs only to the sufferer.

The family may feel shocked that their child has an eating disorder or grieved over how their family seems to have 'fallen apart' since their child became ill. But blaming oneself or the sufferer will not resolve the situation. It is more constructive to look at what changes need to be made. The parents, and in some cases the siblings, will benefit from seeking help for themselves, to understand in what way their means of relating within the family may be causing problems. They will also need caring support.

Parents inevitably feel guilty, wondering if they are the cause of their child's illness. It is hard when a child doesn't eat, or overeats and is not able to attain control. Food, especially for a mother, relates to her worth as a provider of care and nurturing. When a child refuses to eat it feels like rejection of that care. If the sufferer explains to her parents what is happening as she shuts them out of her world, and the parents have the patience to listen, it will ease the situation. Parents need to acknowledge and confess true guilt, making amendments where necessary, and let go of false guilt.

The sufferer is in need of plenty of affirmation and love. Instead, because of the frustration which family members feel, she is usually on the receiving end of anger and threats. Care should be taken not to punish her for being ill – the distortions in the sufferer's thinking, her lack of communication, irritability, and defensive reactions can be due partly to malnutrition. Parents need to be firm but consistently loving. For the sufferer to be told 'You'll kill yourself' often only tells her what she already knows but doesn't apply to herself, and makes her feel even less understood. Any sense of not being understood causes her to dig her heels in even further. It is more productive to ask the sufferer how family members can help rather than *assume* that they know. One of the most beneficial things a family can do for a sufferer is to understand what she is trying to communicate *through* the eating disorder.

Other responses which will help the sufferer are:

- giving her freedom to make choices
- not persistently pushing her for explanations
- not attempting to control her eating

- not always having to know everything about her
- not treating her differently because of her eating disorder
- not letting her illness dictate to the family
- not failing to build trust just because trust has been shattered through her deceit

As the sufferer faces her eating disorder a necessary part of the process is taking responsibility for herself, appropriate to her age. It is better to encourage her to take responsibility and support her as she struggles to do so than to step in and rescue her. The exception is if she's becoming physically seriously ill and needs to be hospitalised immediately. Parents should try to talk *to* their child rather than *about* her, and encourage her to *speak for herself* rather than *speaking for her*, even if she appears hesitant. It is important not to shield the child from pain, disappointment, or growing up, and not to over-protect her. Sometimes the desire to protect can have more to do with the parents' own need to guard themselves from old hurts or experiencing uncomfortable feelings:

> "A crucial struggle is for parents and children to separate with love. The relationship of parent and child has to be severed and then slowly soothed and healed into something new. As long as parents feel overly responsible for their child, the child will not grow up and face life on its own. The separation is not just a matter of age or geographics. It is a deep emotional commitment and tie which must be broken for survival to occur".[8]

It will help the sufferer if parents are able to face and express their own feelings to each other and allow her to express her feelings, even negative ones, without being judged. Many parents coping with a child who has an eating disorder feel angry. If they can separate the behaviour from the person and feel angry with the eating disorder rather than with the sufferer it will be more constructive. Conflict needs to be expressed and resolved, but it is wise to choose times other than mealtimes.

Being prepared to listen to a sufferer's opinions, even when these differ from the parents', will give her a sense of value and individuality. People can have a contrasting opinion and not be rejecting the other person. Some parents feel that it is not acceptable to express their opinions in case this is met with a negative reaction and 'makes their child worse'. Parents have as much right as the children to express their own opinions. If they do not express their own opinions they may be feeding the sufferer's tendency to manipulate. The only condition to expressing an opinion is that the one doing the expressing does not invalidate the other person's opinion at the same time. It's vital that the sufferer's preferences are acknowledged without always being made to feel these are wrong.

Earlier, in Chapter 5, I mentioned that one of the weaker aspects of the eating disorder family is communication. Open, direct communication is important for the healing of the whole family, not just the sufferer. Dropping hints, leaving notes, using another member of the family as a go-between or saying words out loud which someone is 'meant to overhear' are not healthy means of communication – they destroy us.

Just as parents and siblings need to make changes so may the partners of sufferers. Some of their reactions could be compounding the problem. Sometimes a sufferer marries someone who has carried into the relationship unhealthy relating patterns and unresolved hurts. Peter Lambley, in his study of the partners of six anorexics, found that four had hospital diagnoses: (1.) passive depressive (2.) psychopath (3.) schizophrenic breakdown (4.) drug addict.[9] The partner and sufferer are equal. For one to view the other as a substitute parent, or someone who is going to 'come to the rescue', is not productive.

## Support from friends

Elizabeth wrote to me throughout her illness. Her last letter spoke of how important the support of friends and family had been during her recovery. 'What made all the difference was having people who came to visit me or wrote to me again and again, even when I was belligerent, unresponsive and, in the case of my close family, rude and extremely hurtful'.

Being a friend to someone who is suffering from an eating disorder is not easy. The friendship invariably goes through a time of testing when the person who is not suffering can lose heart or patience as she watches someone for whom she cares destroying herself. Many people walk away, unable to sustain their commitment.

Most valuable in a friendship is understanding about eating disorders: what it's like to have an eating disorder, how the sufferer is feeling and why she needs this means of coping. Understanding is not merely learning the facts about eating disorders, it's imagining oneself inside the sufferer's skin. What would it be like to feel her feelings, have her fears, see the world through her eyes? The choice of words and comments is important: words both wound and heal, pull down and build up. An anorexic or bulimic will find comments about how she has put on weight or how much better she looks hard, and it may reinforce her determination to take control of her body. 'You look your old self again' can be frightening if the sufferer hated herself before the illness. The *new person* who is emerging needs to be affirmed, along with the sufferer's qualities and her efforts towards recovery, rather than her weight gain or loss. Friends, carers and therapists also need to be careful about judgmental attitudes as they are faced with some behaviour. It is essential to see beyond the illness to the *person:*

"While encouraging the sufferer to become more expressive and more accurately aware of how she currently is, it is crucial for the helper to remain tuned to the fact that the sufferer's real self is so tentative and fragile she does not have the resources to cope with even the most minor intrusions. Even talking to her can leave her feeling invaded, exploited, controlled. So it must be made equally clear to her that it is entirely acceptable for her to keep her thoughts, feelings and experiences to herself. She does not have to share them with the helper, and it is important that the helper does not create an obligation, unspoken or otherwise, that she should".[10]

Being real with the sufferer, sharing feelings and allowing her to see that it is acceptable to feel needy and to be vulnerable will help her to do likewise. If she senses that others are hiding things from her, or are unable to express their feelings, she cannot be expected to respond with openness. Personal honesty and empathy also opens the door to the right to confront the sufferer. Gentle, but firm, confrontation will be needed at various points.

Decision-making and doing things for herself can be hard for the sufferer, but other people making decisions and doing things for her remove responsibility and independence – the very things which will bring healing in the long run. If she is struggling she needs to be lovingly helped to move towards accomplishing what she finds difficult. For instance, if she says that she cannot make a phone call, it is more productive for a friend to offer to be with her whilst she makes the call than to make the call for her.

During recovery, affirmation is needed for even the smallest of steps, but the sufferer will find 'healing' being talked about a great deal very threatening. Telling her to 'give it to God' is also likely to make her angry. She is torn in two – a part of her wants to but another part is frightened. It is more helpful for friends to encourage her to discover the *nature* of God, and let her come to her own conclusions about giving areas of her life to Him when she is ready.

## Moving towards recovery

Recovery from an eating disorder is not easy to determine because it depends on a person's definition of recovery. I feel that recovery involves a number of essential factors: maintaining a weight within 10 per cent of average for her age and height; the return of menstruation; a life no longer centred around food and weight; the ability to eat three meals a day without guilt; occasionally overeating or skipping a meal without being tempted to starve, binge or vomit; the ability to maintain work; the establishing of friendships; emotional and physical separation from parents, appropriate to her age; the ability to have fun; acting out of choice not just duty; not exchanging her eating disorder for any other addiction.

Full recovery is possible for every sufferer. Sadly many do not find it because they receive unhelpful, inadequate or insufficient treatment; are not motivated to change; are trapped in circumstances which perpetuate the problem; or do not have the necessary support.

# 9 | OPTIONS FOR HELP

Considering the options for help can be difficult. For some people a combination of help is useful. It may also prove to be beneficial to consider different types of help at the various stages of the eating disorder. In this chapter there is a very brief outline of some of the types of help which are available, but as you consider which option to take it is worth bearing in mind the wise words of one ex-sufferer: 'I began to get well when I took responsibility for my own recovery'.

## Counselling and psychotherapy

Counselling involves caring, listening, prompting, asking questions, and having empathy. Empathy is the ability of the counsellor to see things through the eyes of the sufferer and yet to be objective. Counselling is a relationship of trust. The sufferer needs to trust the counsellor, and to be trusted herself. This is only possible if there is openness and honesty. Gemma found empathy, love, acceptance and honesty were the most powerful aspects of her counselling. 'Without these the insight would have fallen on deaf ears'. The kinds of questions asked help a person to share and to get in touch with her feelings. Counselling explores the current difficulties a person is having, and enables her to understand and deal with the reasons behind her eating disorder. It also helps her to discover healthy ways of coping.

Psychotherapy is similar to counselling but deals at a deeper level, looking closely at the hurts of the past. For therapy to work the sufferer needs to be helped to look at causes, and to express feelings, conflicts and fears, rather than just to talk about the eating disorder. The eating disorder is explored in terms of its purpose for the sufferer. The way she relates and how this is expressed in the therapy sessions forms an important part.

It is said that if an anorexic is at a very low weight, therapy is unlikely to be effective. 'When a person's weight falls to between 70 per cent and 80 per cent of her average expected body weight ... then the characteristic anorexic way of thinking develops and communication problems become severe'. In this situation it is best that she is given support with the chance to share, but not intensive therapy.[1]

Counselling and psychotherapy need to be seen as safe places where the sufferer can allow the buried pain to come out. To feel safe it should be regular. It is a time when she learns to express herself: 'I feel ...', 'I need ...', 'I am ...', 'I fear ...', 'I enjoy ...'.

There is a difference between secular and Christian counselling. Ultimately secular counselling will help a person to find the resources within herself to cope with life, whilst Christian counselling will address the relationship with God as one of the key resources to handling life's difficulties. However, even Christian counselling can vary tremendously from being very similar to secular counselling but with prayer, to being based on biblical principles for living. To me, Christian counselling can only be such if biblical teaching is central to the help being offered. For Naomi, Christian counselling was an indispensable part of her treatment. 'Through this I have learned a lot about myself. I have travelled a long way on my journey towards an understanding and acceptance of myself'.

## Group therapy
Group therapy is similar to individual therapy in exploring underlying causes and helping a sufferer to talk

about her pain. She learns to express anger in the safety of a group of people who understand how she feels, and to use words rather than bingeing, vomiting or starving. Groups usually consist of about eight people, are for a limited number of weeks, and are led by a therapist. People's feelings are explored, as is the way they relate. Sometimes the way a person relates to the group is used as a means of exploring the way she used food. This can be powerful in helping her to look at her behaviour. In discovering how to communicate, the sufferer can learn a pattern which breaks down barriers and helps her to form meaningful relationships.

As people open up, group therapy can be very painful, but as they support each other it can also be very loving. It may be easier to accept confrontation from another sufferer than someone who 'doesn't understand how it feels'. Many sufferers gain through giving help and showing care to other members. Seeing one member express her feelings offers guidelines to another who may struggle. Realising that other people believe in her can enable a sufferer to feel better about herself and see that the past does not have to control her life.

If led effectively one of the strong benefits of group therapy is the sense of belonging and affirmation between members. The group is often seen to be a safe place where people can share openly and honestly with those who truly understand. However, in some groups sharing between the group members outside the group times is actively discouraged as it is said that something is lost if not all group members are present. This can then lead to feelings of isolation and loneliness when not in the group.

## Family therapy
Family therapy is particularly useful if the sufferer is still living at home, since a part of the reason behind the eating disorder is often unresolved issues within the family. The therapist explores the attitudes and behaviour of the

family, and looks at how each member feels about the sufferer's problem.

The purpose is to look at what is happening in the family as a whole, not to lay blame.

For change to take place old patterns need to be altered, which can be very painful. Family values, conflict and communication are explored as well as the way the family resolves problems and the means of nurturing each other. Members are expected to express their *own* opinions. This can create conflict, which may be both unusual and uncomfortable for the family. But if they can learn how to work through the conflict in the sessions it will be beneficial.

Members are helped to develop new communication and relationship skills. They are encouraged to be more flexible and to view each other as separate individuals. Family therapy also helps to change the way the family handles the sufferer's behaviour.

## Hospitalisation

Hospitalisation becomes necessary when a person's weight is very low, she is finding it too difficult to cope with everyday life, or bingeing/vomiting is out of control. Depending on the circumstances, a sufferer may be admitted to a general hospital, on a medical or a psychiatric ward, or to a psychiatric hospital. Some hospitals have an eating disorder unit.

For dangerously underweight patients, weight can be increased by naso-gastric tube, intravenous drip or central feeding line. For some people these can be frightening and nutritional drinks may be used as an alternative. In many cases anti-depressants are used. Appetite stimulants are rarely effective with anorexia since it is the desire to control, not the loss of, appetite which is the problem.

Some hospitals use behaviour modification: rewarding the sufferer when she eats and punishing her when she doesn't. A target weight is set for the patient to achieve before she can be discharged. This treatment can help to put on weight but rarely sorts out the emotional aspects of the problem. If given without psychotherapy or coun-selling it can lead to bulimia, depression or attempted suicide. It can cause the sufferer to feel powerless, and to become manipulative. When Kerry was fifteen she was admitted to the children's ward of a general hospital. She was not allowed to bath or wash her hair for ten days, or to have visitors for three weeks. 'I felt everything I had control over had been removed'. When I was discharged I became obsessive. I would sit for hours trying to find a hairstyle that would not need a comb or clips in case these were suddenly taken from me'.

If a person refuses hospitalisation and her life is considered to be in danger (either medically or by risk of suicide) she may be Sectioned (compulsorily detained) under the 1983 Mental Health Act. This can feel like the ultimate in other people taking control. A person can also be put on a Section when she is already in hospital. Following unsuccessful treatment in a general hospital for anorexia Beverley developed bulimia and was admitted to a psychiatric hospital. The causes of her eating disorder were not being dealt with and she became desperate. 'I used to go out and buy packets of painkillers and razor blades. I had my stomach pumped a couple of times and my arms stitched. Eventually I was put under a Police Section. Someone observed me night and day'. Beverley was protected from killing herself but was not receiving adequate therapy to deal with the bulimia.

The type of treatment a sufferer receives, and the way she is handled, is important. It needs to be a place where her fears are taken seriously, she is shown care, and is encouraged to stand on her own feet. One of the problems with long hospital stays is that the person can become dependent on a safe environment, where she is not having to face everyday pressures. The sufferer should be somewhere where she not only receives medical treatment but, in time, the underlying issues are looked at.

## Therapeutic community

Therapeutic communities can be residential or non-residential and usually have a thorough approach to emotional problems. They are staffed by a mixture of professionals: psychiatrists; psychotherapists; family therapists; occupational therapists; nutritionists and care workers. Generally, they do not take severely underweight or ill patients. One centre[2] describes the kind of person who benefits from being in a therapeutic unit as one having a degree of insight into her problems, being in touch with reality, and motivated to change.

A great deal of information is given about the eating disorder and its consequences. There are morning and afternoon group sessions. Each patient also has an individual therapist and the chance for marital or family therapy. Patients are offered dietary advice but may provide their own lunch. Another centre[3] outlines that eating is not supervised and target weights are not set. The physical aspect is not neglected – all patients receive an extensive physical examination. They may be given anti-depressants or anti-obsessional drugs, but tranquillisers and sedatives are very rarely used. Patients are free to see their notes any time and to write in them. Change is always the responsibility of the patient.

People who received this treatment gained weight at a slower rate than those who had received in-patient hospital treatment but they had fewer weight fluctuations. They also felt more in control of their eating at follow-up[4].

Natasha, talking of the group sessions in the therapeutic community, said:

"Through all the fear and terror I felt something – love and warmth. These people who shouted at each other, laughed and cried together really cared about each other. I'll never forget the moment when I first felt it. I wanted to be in there with them. I have not regretted coming here. There has been a lot of pain, but with it has come a huge change in me. I can now feel the genuine pleasure of being with people who are real, and accept me for me".[5]

Unfortunately, therapeutic communities are few and far between. *Kainos Trust* (the charity which I run) offers residential courses along similar lines to a therapeutic community, except that *Kainos Trust* does not operate on a medical model: the setting is more accurately described as a family setting, making it unique in what it has to offer.

## Art therapy

Art therapy is often seen as a positive form of treatment for eating disorders in that it is non-judgemental. Value is on the *person* rather than on her weight.

For the bulimic or compulsive eater art therapy enables the person to see what she is eating.[6] Her needs, which are pushed down through bingeing, are expressed on paper. It 'can be viewed in part as a means of expressing what cannot be tolerated in words or feelings'.[7] For the anorexic the artwork produced is unique to her as an individual, which can help to show her that she has feelings of her own, even if they are hidden and confused ones.[8] Katy, an eighteen-year-old anorexic, used to paint an image of herself in white paint on white paper, effectively making herself invisible. She felt transparent within her family, with no substance.[9]

Art therapy is non-threatening; the sufferer is in control and can stop at any time. Allowing her to work at her own pace, and in a safe and confined environment, helps the patient to establish trust.[10] One of the most important aspects of art therapy is that the patient must participate in her own treatment, and thereby her own recovery.[11]

Through art many repressed memories can come to the surface, and the sufferer may discover some of the deep causes of her illness.

## Self-help groups

A self-help group is not effective if all people do is talk about food. It exists as a safe place to relieve the isolation and to bring understanding as to how people feel. The aim is not so much to heal the person's pain and conflict, as to help her become aware. That is why it is often necessary to have therapy in addition to attending a group.

The group gives a person the chance to *speak* about how she is feeling instead of *acting it out* through her behaviour. She can practise being assertive in an accepting environment; experiment with expressing her feelings; discover the reasons behind her eating disorder; and begin to develop healthy relationships. Anything personal which is spoken about is confidential. If members do not honour this rule then the group, which is based on trust, will break down. Everyone has the right to remain silent, to be heard, to express and own her feelings.

Anorexics, who have difficulty in admitting they have needs, find it hard to attend self-help groups. Bulimics, with their wanting and yet fearing, often struggle with commitment. Compulsive eaters, who have problems in setting their own boundaries, need structure.

A structured group might consist of each member sharing how their week has been . Following this it can be helpful to have a talk, discussion or therapeutic exercise. Members need to feel that they are *working* on their problems not just *talking* about them. This may be concluded by feeding back how the discussion or exercise was received. The final part of the meeting may be given over to a time of winding down, when people talk about things other than their problems.

For a group to work members must go with the right attitude to recovery, where people are seriously trying to help themselves. It is important that a couple of the members are well-advanced in recovery and more in touch with their feelings, otherwise the group will find it difficult to progress.

## Befriending

Befriending can be used as a means of support for someone who is in therapy, or as an encouragement for someone not yet ready to seek professional help. Facing painful past memories creates strong emotions and leaves the sufferer, at times, feeling very desperate. She needs people who are *committed* to her.

Isobel described her best form of help as 'being loved and understood'. Befrienders are people who offer comfort but also remain objective and help the sufferer to see reality. For a while she may need a surrogate parent who can teach her skills that she failed to learn in childhood. Listening to the words beneath the sufferer's actions and noticing what she *doesn't* say can tell the befriender what is going on for the sufferer.

Befrienders exist as a guide not a crutch; to care not to smother. They can relieve the isolation and exist as people with whom the sufferer can learn to be herself, building confidence for future friendships. Befriending is an art; to be befriended takes practice too. The sufferer may fling her emotions out, or she may test the befriender to see if she cares. Successful befriending is found in communication, honesty and reliability; also loving the person despite her behaviour, although this does not mean that the befriender endorses unhelpful behaviour patterns. Befriending involves coming alongside people, supporting and leading them by example.

## Telephone helplines

Telephone helplines can be useful in times of crisis or moments of loneliness. The main disadvantage is that people may become dependent on them.

Speaking to someone on the phone, who understands eating disorders, can help sufferers to face underlying issues. It will also bridge the gap between denying there is a problem and seeking professional help. Some helplines are specialised, others offer more general help. Some also give the chance to talk face-to-face, or suggest where professional help can be sought. Isobel found the Samaritans very supportive:

"When I first phoned the Samaritans I was fifteen, my parents were separated and my mother had a drink problem. I had not opened up to anyone before, but felt better for doing so. It wasn't easy talking and I felt guilty afterwards. Being listened to helped me to feel less alone. It was a good way of having some contact, but keeping at a safe distance. One day I plucked up the courage to visit the Samaritans. I felt welcomed and free to release my emotions. It was a great source of comfort, but I realise that it is not the ultimate solution".

As Isobel described, helplines can be beneficial but they are not the ultimate solution. They have saved many people's lives, but need to be used wisely. With telephone helplines there is the tendency to seek a quick answer to deep pain or for someone else to sort the problem rather than helping yourself. There can also be the tendency to be supported *in* the eating disorder rather than being equipped to *overcome* it.

## Prayer and healing

Some people have received prayer for an eating disorder and have been instantaneously healed by the power of God. In my experience this is the exception rather than the rule. The reason, I suspect, is that emotional and spiritual growth take place in the recovery process.

Shortly after my book *Puppet on a String* was published

Stephanie, who was anorexic, wrote saying she would like to meet me. I sensed that she needed to ask God to provide someone with whom she could pray regularly. The following week a couple in her church approached her. 'They prayed with me each week and brought words of knowledge about hurts in my life. As these were dealt with I began to experience healing'. Someone passed her a piece of paper on which were written the words:

> "The Lord will guide you always;
>     he will satisfy your needs in a
>         sun-scorched land
>     and will strengthen your frame.
> You will be like a well-watered garden,
>     like a spring whose waters never fail".
> Isaiah 58:11 NIV

This was the beginning of a major change in Stephanie's life and she is now fully recovered.

Many lives have been changed through prayer for the healing of past hurts, restoration of relationships, and release of bitterness. As a person is prayed for, the Holy Spirit can bring back memories long forgotten and heal deep and raw wounds. The sting and crippling effects of rejection which may have taken place very early in life, or even in the womb, can be transformed into something new.

When God gives to someone a word of knowledge about another person it can bring healing in a way that may otherwise take months. Rosie, when facing the effects of sexual abuse, met with a friend. 'God has shown me that I must pray for your hands', the friend said. Rosie was dumbfounded. Only God could have known the dirt she felt attached to her hands as a child. She had even doubted her experience of abuse. God had revealed that He knew it was real!

# 10 | BODY AND NUTRITION

When a person first begins to experience problems with her eating or her weight it is important to see a medical doctor to ensure that there is not a physical cause. Having decided that she wants to work towards recovery, it is also helpful to have regular medical check-ups. The doctor may recommend medication such as anti-depressants. For bulimia, studies show that a high percentage of sufferers have been greatly helped, both with mood swings and vomiting, by the use of carefully selected anti-depressants.[1]

## Making changes

For the anorexic, increasing the amount she is eating can be not only frightening but physically uncomfortable, as her shrunken stomach has to stretch and her body read-just to dietary changes. Raymond Vath, a medical doctor, points out that the amount of food should be increased gradually. Too fast a weight gain can result in bloating, nausea, vomiting and even heart failure.[2] With re-feeding, the anorexic may at first appear bulky around her middle with thin arms and legs, but weight should distribute evenly in time. Her metabolic rate will have slowed down and when she initially increases what she is eating she will put on weight quite fast. As her body adjusts and her metabolic rate increases, her weight-gain will slow down.

The physical effects of poor nutrition begin to right themselves as a sufferer achieves a normal weight. On reaching and maintaining 90 per cent of the correct weight for her age and height an anorexic should start to menstruate within six to nine months. The only things which she might find strange are that she suddenly seems to catch colds, having been fairly resistant to them at a low weight; also her hair may begin to fall out, but this is replaced by new healthy hair in a short time. In moving towards a near normal weight sexual feelings will return, which are often disturbing for the sufferer who has put a halt to puberty. She will need time to adjust to the changes.

At first it is hard for the sufferer not to count the calories in every mouthful. A conscious decision to see food as nourishment, not fat, needs to be made. As life becomes filled with greater meaning, and underlying causes are dealt with, anorexia and bulimia cease to serve a purpose and counting calories begins to diminish.

It is not unusual for a recovering anorexic to go through a period of chaotic eating. Once her body begins to crave food, and she gives in, it can be hard to control the need for food. This is only a phase. One helpful way to prevent eating getting out of control is not to deprive the body of the food it needs. The same applies to the bulimic. If a person misses breakfast, or has only half of what her body really needs at lunch-time, it is likely that once she eats, particularly in the evening, she will be unable to stop. If someone has been anorexic for a long time she can find it difficult to assess how much most people eat and may need someone to show her a normal portion. Similarly, the compulsive eater may have to begin to ask herself whether or not she is *truly* hungry before and during eating.

When the anorexic or bulimic wants to get better it is preferable not to weigh herself at first. Not knowing her weight can help her not to take drastic measures every time there is a slight increase. It will also reduce the obsession with how much she weighs. As with any obsession or compulsion, the more the person carries out her ritual the more she feeds the problem. Although the sufferer does not have to know her weight in the early stages of recovery it is advisable that it is checked regularly by her GP, especially if she is very low in weight or is receiving counselling.

Usually the anorexic has defined a weight which she finds it hard to go above. As Rosie was recovering she can remember feeling that being 7 stone 13 lbs (111 lbs/50.5 kg) was OK but she must not be 8 stone (112 lbs/50.9 kg) Her correct weight for her age and height was 8 stone 12 lbs (124 lbs/56.4 kg). Most anorexics, as they put on a little weight, need to come to terms with being a little heavier before being expected to gain any more weight. It is important for them to have someone to talk to about how they feel concerning the changes. They often experience a greater sense of desperation at this stage than when severely anorexic.

The way food is viewed is important, which may mean letting go of media and peer pressure. The person with an eating disorder needs to begin to look at food not in diet terms or emotional terms, but as nutrition to the brain and body. Although it is hard, recovery involves letting go of dieting and letting go of the war within herself over food. 'War requires at least two sides. When you decide that you will listen to *yourself* and not to your calorie-counter or your fears, there is nothing to rebel against. There is nothing you can't have tomorrow so there is no reason to eat it all today'.[3] One mistake often made is that a person restricts herself in such a way that when she does not stick to her regime she feels she has 'blown it' and might as well stuff herself. The next day she crash diets. On a diet her metabolic rate slows down to cope with the reduced intake of food. Those who repeatedly crash diet will find it harder and harder to lose weight.

For the anorexic or bulimic coming off laxatives will not be easy. Gradually cutting back, rather than just stopping, and increasing her fibre as she does so will help to prevent a feeling of bloatedness and uncomfortable abdominal cramps. Coming off laxatives and stopping vomiting can have some unpleasant effects such as shaking, feeling light-headed and, in some cases, a bit hungover. These are withdrawal symptoms which will pass.

Seriously trying to gain weight requires stopping excessive exercise and keeping warm at all times. The anorexic will need to eat regular meals with healthy snacks between each meal. Though often disliked by anorexics high protein drinks can help, as can milk, milk pudding, bananas, avocados, dried fruit and nuts.

The weight at which anorexia becomes life-threatening depends on age, height, speed at which the weight has been lost, medical complications and the amount of exercise being taken. It is advisable that if the sufferer is 65 per cent of, or below, her expected body weight for her age and height she should be hospitalised, rather than trying to handle the situation at home. If she is desperately underweight and not eating much then it needs to be ensured that her intake includes one glass of orange juice, one glass of milk, one portion of yoghurt and some sunflower seeds each day, in order to protect the electrolyte balance and the bones.

If a person is overweight, and seriously wants to lose weight, healthy eating and regular exercise will help to achieve this. I believe that consistent healthy eating is far better than slimming diets. If a set slimming diet needs to be followed this should be done for a limited period of time and preferably under medical supervision. The goal for the compulsive eater should be not slimness but stopping using food as a means of masking problems, giving relief and comfort, burying anger, hiding fears, filling emptiness or for any other reason. Heckel points out that an overeater cannot be considered cured, even if she loses weight, unless the other symptoms have cleared up. The result will be 'thin fat people',[4] people who may now be thin but are still fat in their mentality. If someone is dieting repeatedly, continuously losing weight then gaining weight over a period of years, then it indicates that they are focusing on the physical rather than the emotional aspects of the problem.

## Creating a food ladder

There will come the day when the sufferer has to make a decision to work at altering her eating patterns. What has become habitual, probably over quite a period of time, will not be changed without some effort from the person. It is good to begin by gradually introducing into her every day diet foods which she considers to be 'bad' or 'threatening', difficult though this may be. If she says 'I must not eat bread' and tries to exclude it , but secretly likes it, then it is highly probable that bread will be one of the foods on which she will binge.

Creating a food ladder can help. The idea behind constructing the food ladder is for the sufferer to focus on the sorts of food which she would like to be able to eat. She must be prepared to confront these foods by including them in her normal intake. For instance, if milk has been on her list of forbidden foods she could try adding it to tea or coffee each day. The foods she particularly dreads are put at the top of the list, those she feels less anxious about at the bottom. She then works her way up the ladder.

1.   A portion of chips
2.   A helping of cream
3.   A slice of cake
4.   Roast potatoes
5.   A piece of chocolate
6.   A portion of cheese
7.   A sweet biscuit
8.   A slice of bread and butter
9.   A slice of bread without butter
10.  A fruit-flavoured yoghurt
11.  A baked potato
12.  A cream cracker biscuit
13.  Milk in tea and coffee[5]

## What about a nutritionist?

It is advisable for all sufferers to seek help from a nutritionist who can assess the most beneficial diet. There are many nutritional factors which may be creating unpleasant symptoms or restricting full recovery. A nutritionist can help detect vitamin and mineral deficiencies and recommend dietary changes and supplements to correct these. There may be further complications which can be sorted out too. Marina, who suffered from anorexia, sought advice from a nutritionist who discovered that she had inherited pyroluria, a stress-related disorder in which zinc and vitamin B6 bind together and are excreted before proper usage.

Another problem is intolerance to certain foods. People who have food intolerances often crave the foods of which they are intolerant, which may perpetuate a binge. Like any addiction they feel they need more in order to avoid the withdrawal symptoms. It is also possible that toxic metals such as lead, copper, aluminium or cadmium may be present and contribute to mental disturbances.

A nutritionist can look at factors which are preventing a person from adequately digesting, absorbing and utilising what is being eaten. She can also detect whether amino acid supplements for someone with anorexia or bulimia would be useful. These help to restore proper function to the metabolic pathways of the brain, and assist in normalising self-perception, enabling the sufferer to want to get better.

## Vitamins and minerals

Common vitamin and mineral deficiencies in people with eating disorders, depending on the nature and severity of the disorder, are:

**Vitamin A**   respiratory infections; scaly skin; poor hair quality; eye problems.

**Vitamin C** dry scaly skin; gum problems; haemorrhaging in skin, eyes, nose; muscle and joint pains.

**Vitamin D** aching legs; muscular weakness and spasms; brittle bones.

**Vitamin E** lethargy; muscle weakness; lack of concentration; decreased sexual interest.

**Vitamin B1** muscle weakness; tender calves; fatigue; digestive upsets; loss of appetite; nausea; impaired concentration; irritability; depression; poor memory.

**Vitamin B2** gritty, sensitive, bloodshot eyes; cracked corners of mouth; sore tongue; scaly skin on face; hair loss; insomnia; dizziness.

**Vitamin B6** similar skin and mouth problems; migraine; irritability; depression; breast tenderness; swollen abdomen, fingers and ankles.

**Vitamin B12** menstrual disorders; symptoms of anaemia; nervous problems.

**Magnesium** low blood sugar; muscle cramps and tremors; involuntary eye movements; heart rhythm problems; difficulty swallowing; weakness; dizziness and convulsions; nervousness.

**Potassium** drowsiness and confusion; intense thirst and loss of appetite; abdominal distension; vomiting; low blood pressure; muscular weakness; pins and needles; paralysis.

**Calcium** bone and muscle problems similar to vitamin D deficiency.

**Iron**   anaemia.

**Zinc**   white spots on nails; eczema; impaired sense of taste or smell; susceptibility to infections; hair loss; mental apathy.[6]

Sources of vitamins and minerals are:

**Vitamin A**
- lamb's/chicken liver
- eggs
- carrots
- dark green vegetables
- sweet potatoes
- cantaloupe melon
- apricots
- cheese
- margarine
- herrings
- mackerel
- sardines
- salmon
- tuna
- eggs

**Vitamin C**
- oranges
- grapefruit
- melon
- strawberries
- raspberries
- gooseberries
- blackcurrants
- lemons
- potatoes
- watercress
- tomatoes
- green/red peppers
- runner beans
- fresh/frozen peas
- cabbages
- cauliflowers
- brussel sprouts

**Vitamin D**
- milk

**Vitamin E**
- seeds
- seed oils
- wheatgerm
- corn
- peanuts
- almonds
- mayonnaise
- soya beans

**B Vitamins**
- wheatgerm
- wholegrains
- seeds
- nuts
- green vegetables
- pulses (peas, beans, lentils)
- milk, milk products
- liver
- eggs

## Vitamin B3
- meat
- poultry
- fish
- wholegrain products
- nuts
- pulses (peas, beans, lentils)

## Vitamin B6
- lamb's liver
- chicken
- fish
- eggs
- leeks
- kale
- hazelnuts

## Vitamin B6 and Magnesium
- avocados
- bananas
- cabbages
- cauliflowers
- sweet peppers
- brown rice
- brewers yeast
- sunflower seeds
- beef

## Magnesium
- apples
- blackberries
- grapes
- dried fruit
- figs
- lemons

- grapefruit
- parsley
- brazil/cashew nuts
- chicken
- cheese
- sesame seeds
- jacket potatoes
- aubergines
- broccoli
- carrots
- celery
- peas
- green beans
- mushrooms
- onions
- iceberg lettuce
- sweetcorn
- tomatoes

## Potassium
- vegetables (especially cabbages, carrots, celery)
- tomatoes
- fruits (especially apples, bananas, oranges, grapefruit, avocados)
- dried fruit
- nuts
- dandelion coffee

## Calcium
- milk
- hard cheese
- yoghurt
- sesame seeds
- soya flour

- kelp
- green leafy vegetables
  (not spinach)

**Iron**
- lamb's/chicken liver
- molasses
- shellfish
- sardines
- beans
- wholemeal bread
- wheatgerm
- figs
- apricots

- prunes
- almonds

**Zinc**
- seafoods
- meat
- lamb's liver
- eggs
- wholegrain cereals
- wheatgerm
- almonds
- seeds
- sprouted grains
  (especially wheat)[7]

## Hypoglycaemia

A sufferer may have low blood sugar in response to bingeing on sugary foods. One of the causes of feeling hungry between meals can also be a fluctuation in blood sugar (glucose) levels:

> "All our starch and sugar are changed to glucose by the process of digestion, because glucose is the form in which carbohydrates can be taken into the bloodstream and transported to all parts of the body, including the brain, and used for energy production. A hormone called insulin, produced by the pancreas, has the function of controlling the uptake of glucose from the bloodstream into the cells where it is needed. But this process can go wrong. If we consistently eat sugar the pancreas is constantly stimulated to produce insulin. This is true with any refined carbohydrate food, but most acutely with sweet things, for which digestion is rapid and glucose enters the bloodstream in a rush. Then the pancreas can over-react and produce too much insulin. The blood glucose takes a rapid drop and may end up too low for normal func-

tioning. This condition is known as hypoglycaemia. If the overstimulation happens too often the pancreas becomes exhausted and then instead of producing too much insulin it produces too little. In that case too much glucose remains in the bloodstream and that is called hyperglycaemia, which in its most severe form is diabetes".[8]

Symptoms of hypoglycaemia include:

- weakness
- faintness
- palpitation
- fast heartbeat
- anxiety, cold sweats , panic attacks
- irritability
- insomnia (especially night waking and nocturnal fridge raiding)
- hunger, nausea
- vertigo
- behaviour problems and mood swings
- mental disturbance
- allergic reactions
- epilepsy in susceptible individuals
- migraine and headaches
- personality disorders (hysteria, hypochondriasis)

Symptoms are worse at mid-morning and mid-to-late afternoon, usually two to five hours after food. One of the commonest contributory factors is excess intake of refined carbohydrates (white products). It is wrong to take sugar to relieve the symptoms. Although sugar relieves the symptoms for a while it encourages a vicious circle: a low blood sugar; refined carbohydrate ingestion; excessive insulin secretion; followed by low blood sugar. One approach for treatment is elimination of refined carbohydrates and eating small frequent meals.[9]

## Pre-menstrual tension

PMT is sometimes a contributory factor to bulimia and compulsive eating. Bingeing is frequently worse in the ten days leading up to menstruation. People who suffer from PMT can be caught in a frightening web of physical and emotional symptoms.

| Physical | Emotional |
|---|---|
| • headache | • anxiety |
| • backache | • confusion |
| • bloating | • tearfulness |
| • weight gain | • mood swings |
| • breast tenderness | • depression |
| • muscle and joint pain | • irritability |
| • craving for sweets | • suicidal thoughts |
| • constipation | • anger |
| • fatigue | • social withdrawal |
| • thirst | • inability to cope |

A number of factors can contribute to PMT; some are physical whilst others are emotional. Gynaecological and hormonal problems may play their part, as do diet, lack of exercise and environmental pollutants. Unresolved conflict, stress and disturbed sleep may exacerbate the condition.

For the ten days leading up to menstruation if the sufferer avoids sugar, refined carbohydrates, salty foods and coffee; eats regularly; takes gentle exercise; takes evening primrose oil and vitamin B6 supplements she may find it relieves some of the symptoms. Other dietary changes and recommended dosages of supplements can be given by a nutritionist.

## Keeping healthy

The more a person puts normal eating patterns into practice the easier they become. At first the anorexic and bulimic may fear their eating is getting out of control. The compulsive eater may fear feeling hungry or empty. Keeping healthy involves various changes. These in themselves should not become an obsession, but merely guidelines.

**Meals**. Eat three meals a day and do not skip breakfast. This helps to stabilise blood sugar levels. Do not allow the body to become too hungry.

**Snacks**. Many people need snacks mid-morning or afternoon. Choose fruit, yoghurt, crackers and low-fat cheese, rather than sweet foods with their blood sugar complications.

**Protein**. Eat more fish and poultry rather than red meat. Include other forms of protein, such as beans and pulses, which are full of fibre. Proteins should account for 12 per cent of our calories per day.

**Complex carbohydrates**. Do not omit carbohydrates. Carbohydrates, in moderation, are essential for the body's functioning. We should get 40 to 45 per cent of our calories from complex carbohydrates, which are potatoes with their skins on, wholegrain rice, whole-wheat flour, oats, etc. Avoid refined (white) products.

**Sugar carbohydrates**. The rest of our carbohydrates come from sugars. Ideally this should be the sugar which occurs naturally in the fruit we eat (fructose) and should not amount to more than 15 per cent of calories per day. Avoid sugar and sugar substitutes as much as possible.

**Fats**. It is not good to cut out all fats. We need essential fatty acids, which are found in uncooked sunflower, safflower and linseed oils. A deficiency can lead to infections and a weakening of the immune system. Some vitamins are only utilised by our bodies if we are taking some fat as part of our food. If fats are not eaten then the person will become short of vitamins A, D, E and K. Oily fish can help reduce cholesterol levels and the risk of heart attacks and strokes. Fats should amount to no more than 30 per cent of calories per day.

**Fruits and vegetables**. Eat plenty of fresh fruit and vegetables, which are an excellent source of fibre, vitamins and minerals. Wash but preferably do not peel them as most of the goodness lies just under the skin.

**Salt**. Keep intake of salt low and do not use when cooking vegetables.

**Beverages**. Avoid coffee and strong tea. Include herbal teas and un-sweetened drinks.

**Alcohol**. Keep alcohol to a minimum.

**Water.** Drink plenty of filtered or bottled water.

**Supplements**. Take a multi-vitamin and mineral supplement with food daily.

**Exercise**. Take regular gentle exercise.

**Preparing meals**. Avoid nibbling at food when preparing.

**Shopping**. Try not to go shopping when hungry, which may result in buying binge foods.

By eating adequate amounts of whole foods, but little sugar, and by taking regular exercise the sufferer is much more likely to keep to her correct weight.

# 11 | *FACING TOUGH FEELINGS*

Getting in touch with emotions and working through past pain is difficult but essential for healing and freedom. It can be a bit like thawing out. God meeting the sufferer in her pain is very powerful and, as she turns to Him and faces the hurts, the sting of the wounds diminishes. The sufferer needs to recognise different feelings when they arise and to find new ways of coping; to discover and work through childhood trauma which has been carefully locked away. With the help of a therapist she can look at the meaning of her eating disorder in terms of feelings and needs.

**Anorexia**. Numbing feelings and denying needs.

**Bulimia**. Splitting off negative feelings and admitting needs, but not being able to hold onto them.

**Compulsive eating**. Pushing feelings down and fearing that her needs will never be met.

Recovery involves reaching a state of being able to admit that it's OK to have needs; to discover, feel and handle them. For an understanding of what some of the needs might be, read Chapter 7 again. It is also helpful if the sufferer can realise which feelings and needs are being met or blocked through her starving or bingeing. She also has to learn to make a connection between her feelings and needs, such as:

**Need** – to give and receive love.

**If fulfilled** – closeness; harmony; intimacy; belonging; togetherness; warmth; affection.

**If unmet** – sadness; pain; longing; emptiness; rejection; loneliness.

**Need** – to make choices.

**Positive feelings connected** – power; strength; enthusiasm; determination; energy; fulfilment; satisfaction; elation.

**If blocked** – frustration; impatience; helplessness; irritation; fury; outrage; anger.[1]

An important part of the healing process is discovering where the pain of unmet needs is coming from – usually it is childhood hurts. Lauren went to boarding school when she was seven. As a young adult she experienced deep emotional pain which she could only describe as 'being torn to shreds'. In therapy she began to realise that she felt hungry for affection – to be hugged. The need had stemmed from separation from her parents and lack of touch.

Along the recovery journey there comes the discovery that the sufferer is a relational being, and so a part of her needs can only be met through meaningful relating to other people. As an adult, *she* must be responsible for making healthy choices in meeting her needs – people cannot be expected to guess what she longs for. Needs cannot be met through people alone: there is a part which *only* God can satisfy. Elizabeth gave her life to Jesus part way through her recovery: 'When I made this commitment I realised that I was never designed to meet my own needs'.

## The way feelings are viewed

The sufferer has a tendency to judge her emotions: 'I shouldn't feel this way because ...', 'Feeling angry is bad'. If she wants to make progress she needs to change the way feelings are viewed. Feelings are not 'good' or 'bad', only 'comfortable' or 'uncomfortable'. She must discover that it's OK to admit vulnerability, cry, feel sad, feel angry, or disagree, so long as these can be expressed in a way which does not intentionally hurt her or anyone else. All feelings need to be acknowledged and valued as a part of the person. The best way to become comfortable with expressing feelings is to practise.

If the sufferer is afraid of her pain it is important that someone is able to sit with her, giving her the message that her feelings can be tolerated by another person and so can also be tolerated by her. We all need the sense that there is someone who understands how we feel. But other people are not there to relieve us of pain, only to help us work through it. We will always experience hurt in life to some degree, and once we stop looking for a pain-free life then pain becomes less feared. Sadly, 'most people never touch the bottom of their pain. They become compulsive instead ...'.[2]

Each member of the family must take responsibility for his or her emotions. Other people do not *cause* us to have certain feelings; we have those feelings in *response* to situations. Instead of saying '*You* make me feel angry ...' try to rephrase it 'I feel angry when you ...'. Owning feelings and not blaming them on someone else takes time.

## The struggle to get in touch

'Getting to know your feelings is part of getting to know yourself as a unique person'[3] but most sufferers struggle to know how they feel. There are various ways of helping someone to get in touch with her feelings.

**Art.**   In therapy Rosie often used the word 'crushed'. Her therapist encouraged her to draw what being crushed was like. Rosie drew several pictures: 1. A body with a black hand pressing down on her chest; 2. A heart broken in two, one half black the other red, surrounded by arrows; 3. A black stick-man separated from a group of red, green and blue stick-men; 4. A very thin stick-man lying under layers and layers of black lines. Without her realising it, black showed up in each picture. It was also the colour she had used to indicate where the pain was on her body as a child, in a drawing the previous week. Her therapist asked her to name each picture. Rosie chose: 1. Pressure; 2. Broken; 3. Separate; 4. Heaviness. She was gradually learning about her feelings. Drawing feelings and talking about them is sometimes easier than just talking.

**Role-play.** Jane was asked by her group therapist to draw a picture of a dream. She drew a large ape, some smaller apes and a little child crying in a crib. Jane was then asked if she would be willing to act out her dream with other members of the group. She chose to play the little child. As the ape approached the child Jane suddenly grabbed her lower abdomen stating that she felt faint and didn't want to go on. She started crying. Later, after she had done another painting, it came out that she had been sexually abused by an older boy when she was much younger.[4] Role-play can be very effective in bringing feelings and blocked memories to the surface and re-creating traumatic scenes, but with a positive outcome.

**Words.** Part of the reason people focus on food and weight is because they are unable to identify and express what is going on inside them. They may talk about 'pain' but be unable to identify the exact feelings. If feelings are not identified they remain unexpressed and can continue to cause difficulties. In helping people to identify how they feel it can be beneficial to give them a list of different feelings (around 200). They can then be encouraged to identify a feeling each day by choosing a word from the list. It may be that later, becoming accustomed to their feelings, they realise that they have not chosen the most suitable word and may opt for another.

**Illustrations.**   Sometimes a person is unable to find the words to describe how she feels. When dealing with someone who is very out of touch with her feelings it is possible to use illustrations. Some illustrations have words to describe the feelings, others are more abstract (see faces pp. 132–133).[5] These are merely tools to help the sufferer to identify with a particular picture which portrays a mood. She can then go on to talk about the illustration and, when she is ready to be helped, to personalise what she is describing.

**The body.**   Learning to listen to the body helps a person to know how she is feeling. Lauren had much buried anger but was unable to recognise it. When she was asked how her body felt as she remembered the incident of being bullied at school she was aware of a tightness in her jaw, clenched fists and a stabbing pain in her chest. Gradually she began to recognise this as anger. Several years later, in therapy dealing with the long-term effects of bullying and sexual abuse, she recognised anger and said that she wanted to kick. The therapist encouraged her to lie down and placed a duvet on her. Pressing on the duvet the therapist expected Lauren to push it off with her feet. Instead she started to sob and turned away, hiding her face. She felt that she could not move. 'Where has the anger gone?' the therapist asked. Lauren pointed to her chest. The parts of her body which had been abused as a child began to hurt. She was able to begin to deal with the pain associated with the trauma. A person can be taught to notice changes in her body and use this as a way of recognising how she feels.

| | | | | |
|---|---|---|---|---|
| aggressive | agonized | anxious | apologetic | arrogant |

| | | | | |
|---|---|---|---|---|
| bashful | blissful | bored | burn-out | cautious |

| | | | | |
|---|---|---|---|---|
| cold | concentrating | confident | curious | demure |

| | | | | |
|---|---|---|---|---|
| determined | disappointed | disapproving | disbelieving | disgusted |

| | | | | |
|---|---|---|---|---|
| distasteful | eavesdropping | ecstatic | enraged | envious |

| | | | | |
|---|---|---|---|---|
| exasperated | exhausted | frightened | frustrated | grieving |

| | | | | |
|---|---|---|---|---|
| guilty | happy | horrified | hot | hungover |

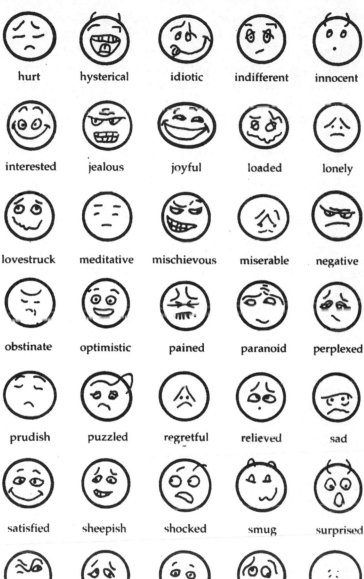

| | | | | |
|---|---|---|---|---|
| hurt | hysterical | idiotic | indifferent | innocent |
| interested | jealous | joyful | loaded | lonely |
| lovestruck | meditative | mischievous | miserable | negative |
| obstinate | optimistic | pained | paranoid | perplexed |
| prudish | puzzled | regretful | relieved | sad |
| satisfied | sheepish | shocked | smug | surprised |
| suspicious | sympathetic | thoughtful | undecided | withdrawn |

**Writing.**   Like drawing, writing feelings down can some-times be easier than talking. Sufferers often keep journals about how much or how little they have eaten. It is more constructive to keep a journal of feelings. When there is a feeling of intense pain it can seem as if the pain will never end, and the person may not understand why she is expe-riencing such hurt. The decision to put pen to paper often leads to hurts and memories being expressed and the sufferer feeling better for having released some of the tension.

When a person is on her own and has gone back to facing childhood hurts she can be screaming inside. It is the child that *was* which is hurting and needing to communicate. It may be helpful to create a dialogue between the child and the adult. Taking a coloured pen in her normal writing hand the sufferer can ask the child questions. Then taking a different coloured pen in her other hand the child can answer.[6] This is a very powerful tool for bringing out suppressed feelings and for creating a sense of protecting and caring for the wounded part of her, without looking to other people to meet that need.

**Listening.**   To listen to other people expressing their feel-ings, especially grief and disappointment, can help a sufferer to identify how *she* feels. In a group therapy setting a sufferer often hears another's words and begins to realise 'that's how I felt when I was little'. As she is faced with the truth about what was lacking as a child, or hears a similar trauma recounted, a surge of feelings may begin to surface.

All these means of getting in touch with feelings are best done under the guidance of a therapist. The more a sufferer allows herself to *feel* her feelings the less scary it becomes to have feelings.

## The need for expression
Just talking about hurts does not release the pain; the

sufferer needs actually to *feel* and *express* her emotions. There are three levels of expression of feelings. The first is to notice and acknowledge what is going on. The second is verbal expression: 'I feel hurt'. The third involves the physical release of feelings – through tears, shouting or trembling.[7]

Something which often holds people back from expressing the pain of childhood is that they are concerned that it will hurt their parents. Facing any pain, or facing the truth, is not comfortable for the sufferer or her family, but she owes it to herself to get sorted out. If she doesn't face childhood hurts it could be more damaging to the relationship with her parents than burying hurts for her parents' protection. Freedom from her eating disorder must become more important than approval from her parents.

A part of the eating disorder has been denying feelings associated with traumatic events. All traumatic events have appropriate feelings attached to them, for instance:

- being bullied – anger and hurt
- death of someone close – grief
- broken trust – anger and sadness
- rape – fear and anger.

If the sufferer gives an account of traumatic events as though totally unrelated to her, and says she did not have any feelings, she will continue to deal with her pain through her eating disorder or equally unhealthy patterns. It is essential to break through the barrier of denial and admit 'I felt ...', 'I feel ...'.

## Particularly troublesome feelings

There are many feelings which will need to be looked at, but the ones which seem most relevant to eating disorders are guilt, fear, anger and grief. The first two the sufferer is often in touch with, the second two, not.

**Guilt.** One sufferer might describe guilt as a general sense of dis-ease, whilst another may experience it as deathly condemnation. Guilt can be a way of prompting the conscience to realise that something is wrong, or it can be a thief come to destroy inner peace. A person my be carrying around true guilt or false guilt. True guilt is a feeling which occurs when that person has violated a law or standard. The guilt fits the action and can be dealt with only by repentance and forgiveness. False guilt comes from an over-sensitive conscience and does not fit the action. It can stem from a person's upbringing or personality.

If the sufferer was brought up in an environment where standards were very high, where there was little encouragement or affirmation, where she was constantly criticised or felt a failure, then adulthood will have brought with it the tendency to respond to failure with crippling self-criticism or guilt. False guilt can also arise out of not accepting the forgiveness which God offers. Resolving false guilt involves dealing with the root of the over-sensitive conscience and distorted thinking, setting realistic standards, reaching a place of self-acceptance, and being able to receive God's forgiveness.

**Fear.** Fear is an emotion people experience when there is a threat to their well-being. The anorexic who fears gaining weight feels that there is a threat to her well-being inasmuch as weight gain will take away the numb, dead feeling and sense of achievement which enables her to survive the hardships of life.

Some of the sufferer's behaviour will be feeding her fears. For example if, because of a fear of failure, she chooses not to participate unless she is sure of coming top, then she may become increasingly fearful of failure.

Some unhelpful fears stem from childhood encounters or from a lack of love and acceptance. Fear of abandonment and rejection are common fears. Felicity said that she often felt a searing pain. As a child her mother found it hard to express love and affection towards Felicity, and her father was always buried in work. She was teased at school and began to feel alone and different. Her wounds led her to believe that people could not be trusted.

To help face her fears the sufferer can:

- identify the different fears and write down everything about them
- deal with any childhood events or words which might have been a building block for the fear
- create in the mind a scenario which builds up to facing one of the fears. For instance, if afraid to go in a lift imagine:

    1. looking at pictures of lifts
    2. asking someone about the safety of lifts
    3. standing outside a lift
    4. going up in a lift one level with a friend
    5. going up in a lift one level alone
    6. going up in a lift more than one level alone

- imagine the worst thing that could happen and decide on a plan of action as to how to cope
- put into practice for real the imagined scenario, committing each stage to God
- understand the extent of God's love. 'There is no fear in love; perfect love drives out all fear'. (1 John 4:18 GNB)[8]

**Anger.** Anger is a secondary emotion. Behind it lie feelings of hurt, frustration or being threatened. Often the sufferer has been afraid of expressing anger because she fears losing control, losing someone's friendship, being rejected or felt shame when angry.

Anger which is expressed against real injustice is not wrong, but what we do with our anger can lead to wrong. To use anger constructively, the sufferer needs to direct the energy behind the anger towards *solving* the problem rather than directing it at others or at herself. If she looks only at the problem, and not the solution, then it is easy to fall into self-pity. Dealing with anger requires admitting that she is angry, discovering what is fuelling the anger and considering whether it is justified or not. If it is not justified then it should be confessed; if it is, then it needs to be expressed through writing, drawing, words or tears.

**Grief.** Recovery involves a grieving process. The five stages of grief are:

- denial
- anger turned outward
- anger turned inward
- genuine sorrow
- resolution and acceptance[9]

Grief exists because there is, or has been, loss. Loss often lies behind depression and inner pain. Loss will also be associated with letting go of the eating disorder. To find healing, the sufferer has to feel and face the various losses in her life. There can be loss of many things, such as:

- innocence
- trust
- protection
- personal opinions
- spontaneity
- love
- touch
- self-esteem
- friends
- being parented
- identity

Only if the person is fully able to express her sorrow will she eventually be able to reach a place of acceptance of all that has happened. Even if the loss is in connection with events which occurred a long time ago, if the pain of the loss has not been acknowledged then the person will not have been through a grief process. Grieving any kind of loss hurts but it is healing. The Psalms remind us: 'Weeping may go on all night, but in the morning there is joy' (Psalm 30:5 TLB). It is this hope and light which she must carry into the dark places she explores.

### Trauma and the child inside

Getting in touch with anger and grief will mean getting in touch with the child inside. When someone has been through trauma – especially physical, emotional or sexual abuse – it is as though part of that child remains frozen within them. This often frightened, needy, angry and hurt little child gradually needs to be faced in the safety of therapy. The trauma does not have to be deep to cause a person to be in terrible pain. For very sensitive people what, to others, may be considered minor can feel devastating.

When Wendy first had memories of her experiences of incest she felt as though she was a child. When she talked about her experience her voice was that of a child. 'I found myself hugging a pillow and rocking to and fro. I also started to sleep with my teddy bear and to cry like a child. When I wrote down how I was feeling it was in childish writing and spelling'.

The sufferer needs to take notice of the cries of the child inside. She needs to go back to the source of the pain and not only feel it but honour it; to know that the hurt child who buried everything is being heard. She must learn to take care of the child inside as a loving parent, rather than looking to other people to parent the child.[10] As she deals with the pain and takes care of the child, the child inside will need to merge with the adult self. This usually requires skilled therapy.

When the child inside initially emerges, and needs to be

faced, the person may find that her eating becomes more chaotic: her eating is designed to keep the child locked away. It can be very hard to handle the pain and still keep going. When the person is not being supported, hurting herself or even suicide may be considered. Lauren was encouraged by her therapist to do the opposite of what she would normally have done when faced with flashbacks of childhood trauma. Her usual pattern was to punish herself by staying outside in the freezing cold for hours at night. Her therapist suggested she should nurture her hurt child – wrap her up in a warm blanket, give her a hot drink and then draw and write about her feelings.

If the sufferer is not helped to deal with the child inside, with the guidance of someone who knows how to deal with this aspect of her, the child will keep making itself known. Lauren's craving to be loved and nurtured, which stemmed from childhood, came out in the pattern of acting-out suicide attempts. She would pretend to take overdoses or take only enough tablets to cause slight drowsiness. She would then put herself in a place where someone would notice her. She liked the feeling of the other person being worried and crying out for her to stay awake. It became a compulsion and an addiction: all she could think about was the warm feeling of being rescued. She had been abused as a child and, once again, she was setting herself up to be the victim. Lauren had planned to 'test' her therapist and to create a victim/rescue scene in her next session. Before she had the chance the therapist started asking her about how many times she had been to hospital. The truth about the scenarios came out.

It was a major change in Lauren's life as she faced the truth and found someone who understood why she did these things. Her therapist explained that what was happening arose out of the child part of Lauren trying to get her needs met. This was her *behaviour* and not Lauren as a person – her behaviour could change. What was happening was that a battle was taking place. Out of her abuse as a child had grown two behaviour patterns – victim and abuser. They constantly fought each other. The victim was the part which felt helpless, powerless, wounded; the abuser was the part which beat Lauren over the head every time she did not match up to her expectations, the part which sabotaged and wounded herself. Somewhere between the two was Lauren as a real person, who had little space to reveal herself. Lauren, the person, was gentle, caring and loved people. She had to learn how to nurture herself rather than continue with the dramatic scenarios. It was a long, slow process but it was the road to healing.

In order to work through feelings the sufferer has to face the truth of the impact of painful events. Many people will deny that childhood hurts were as bad as they were, as a way of keeping their life together. To admit that something was terrible means taking the risk of falling to pieces. Whatever the event, for freedom, the person needs to reach the point of admitting 'It was terrible and I did not like it'. In therapy, safeguards might need to be built into the sessions to make it secure enough for her to look at her pain and anger. This could be an agreement not to damage herself; not to binge and vomit during x-number of weeks, the time at which the pain and anger are being explored. After feeling pain and grieving loss the sufferer needs to be prepared to move on and start the process of letting go of past hurts. The memories will never go completely but they will no longer be dictating to the person. The way she views her pain will change.

Pain does not have to be negative, it can be a strength – it builds empathy with others and changes our characters. We must stop seeing pain as an enemy and start seeing it as a tool.

# 12 | *Making wise choices*

Making choices, let alone wise ones, can be hard for the sufferer. Her recovery is not a clinical process, where she suddenly moves from exploring her feelings to facing her behaviour – she may return to exploring her feelings as others arise. As she begins to look at her behaviour and make changes it can be helpful for the sufferer to set goals. It is useful to list in order of priority what she would like to change, and to be sure that she has short-term and long-term goals which are realistic.

*Exploring behaviour*
Honesty is a prerequisite for change. Exploring behaviour only becomes beneficial when it leads to change, and change only becomes possible where there is honesty. Honesty means the sufferer asking herself questions about her eating disorder, such as:

- what percentage of time does it occupy?
- what else could fill that time?
- is it a means of communicating anything to anyone?
- in what ways is it presenting problems?
- when does it seem worse?
- what are the possible triggers?

Before she can recover, the sufferer has to understand herself and her eating disorder; she cannot change what she does not know. She will also need to begin to make a connection between her feelings and her behaviour:
    'How do I behave when I am feeling … ?'

- angry = withdrawal and starving
- guilty = excessive exercise
- lonely = bingeing

Reactions will vary from person to person and may be different for the same person at different times. When she has built up a good picture of her reactions the sufferer can look at what some of the alternatives are – if she doesn't binge in response to being lonely what else could she choose to do?

The sufferer rarely feels that she has a choice with her behaviour, but she does. The more she has explored the purpose that her eating disorder serves and worked through childhood hurts, the greater her awareness of choice. As a child she was a victim of other people's actions or of circumstances which wounded her; as an adult she has a choice as to how she handles her pain. Victor Frankl, a psychiatrist, makes the point that we are choosing beings. We can't always choose our circumstances, but we can always choose our responses.[1] The sufferer has the choice to stay a victim or to look at her pain and her counter-productive means of coping.

*Breaking down defences*
People who have not faced their pain often repeat with others the very behaviour patterns which have hurt them; or re-enact their past in other relationships, hoping to change the ending to a happier outcome. It is useful to be aware of possible triggers which send a sufferer into these patterns. Many behaviours are developed to escape the reality of how painful life is, but as someone once said: 'If only we realised that the indirect way we choose in order to avoid pain is just as painful as the pain we try so skilfully to avoid … '[2] The breakthrough in recovery comes when the sufferer recognises, and chooses to do something about, unhealthy patterns.

As a child the sufferer may have played certain roles in her family, such as:

**Hero** – keeps the family functioning

**Scapegoat** – the black sheep

**Mascot** – the family clown

**Lost child** – the loner

While the hero is excelling, the scapegoat is getting into scrapes and the mascot is goofing around, the lost child simply isn't noticed. All families have members who play these roles to some extent. In families from which people with eating disorders come other roles may also be adopted:

**Enabler** – covers up the family problem

**Placater** – believes she will make it all better somehow

**Martyr** – will pay any price to alleviate the family situation

**Rescuer** – is going to salvage the situation

**Persecutor** – says: 'It's all your fault'

**Victim** – believes she could be happy if all this weren't happening

These roles are put into practice to survive difficult family situations. When they are continued into adulthood and carried into other relationships they are warped ways of relating which fail to help a person to cope with the world outside.[3]

As she moves towards adulthood the sufferer will have built up defences in order to protect herself from pain, avoid anxiety and stop facing responsibility. Whilst these defences can seem helpful at times they will have created distortion of the real problems and kept other people at a distance. There are many different defences but let us explore those which most often relate to eating disorders.

**Denial** – attempting to minimise the impact of painful events by not acknowledging them or not facing up to reality

**Repression** – burying pain, memories or unacceptable thoughts in the unconscious

**Suppression** – burying pain, memories or unacceptable thoughts in the subconscious

**Intellectualisation** – dealing with a situation by thinking and talking in a detached manner and pushing aside the emotional aspect

**Regression** – going back to feeling and behaving like a child

**Projection** – blaming feelings on someone else

**Rationalisation** – justifying why things are done and the tendency to make excuses

**Reaction formation** – showing to an extreme extent the opposite of how she feels

**Fantasy** – day-dreaming or imaginary achievements

**Manipulation** – controlling other people or directing things in the way she wants them to go to prevent herself feeling uncomfortable

**Withdrawal** – choosing to isolate herself in case of being hurt.

The sufferer needs to begin to look at how these defences may be hindering her from a fulfilling life or a depth of relating which creates a sense of belonging. She can hide the wounded part of her from herself and others with her defences but she cannot hide it from God: 'O Lord, you have examined my heart and know everything about me ... When far away you know my every thought ... You know what I am going to say before I even say it' (Psalm 139:1-2, 4 TLB).

Dropping her defences can be uncomfortable because it means living with times of pain. But if the sufferer is going to grow spiritually, mature emotionally and honestly face her pain in a way which brings healing she must challenge her defences. 'Search me, O God, and know my heart; test my thoughts. Point out anything you find in me that makes you sad, and lead me along the path of everlasting life' (Psalm 139: 23-24 TLB).

Changing patterns comes firstly through honesty, then vulnerability, openness, reaching out in love, forgiveness, patience, and being accountable for her actions and attitudes.

## *Relating and communicating*
All people with eating disorders have difficulties in making and sustaining relationships. These may be apparent, as with the anorexic who rejects contact with other people, or less obvious. The compulsive eater often has many friends and acquaintances but not one really gets close to her or can really help her to meet her needs. She uses people compulsively, in the way she uses food, but fails to feel satisfied by either. The bulimic may easily make relationships and can temporarily feel valued but underneath she feels alone and rejected, sure that no one really cares or can help her.[4]

The ability to master life and handle relationships is

frightening, especially for the anorexic. She can be manipulative but rarely does a controlling approach help. To overcome her sense of powerlessness she needs people who will encourage her to face life and build friendships; people who are willing to stick by her despite her tendency to push away, use or withdraw.

Feeling supported by one or two people she trusts, or in therapy, creates the safety for the sufferer to look at her ways of relating which may be hindering friendships. It is helpful to list and personalise these, for example:

1. 'I always have to be right'
2. 'If I'm criticised I find a way to end the friendship'
3. 'I don't share my feelings'
4. 'I'm always on the defensive'
5. 'I test people to see the extent of their care'
6. 'If I feel misunderstood I withdraw rather than communicate'

There may be specific patterns she can begin to observe.

**1. Looking to others to protect her.** Whilst it is natural to want protection, if the sufferer is looking to other people for protection from childhood wounds she will never feel satisfied. The solution lies within her own ability to care for herself and the knowledge of God's love. This does not mean she has no need of people, but that she ceases to rely on them in order to feel good.

**2. The need for approval.** Approval can be so important to her that the sufferer puts up with things in order not to upset others. If she does not take the risk of disagreement and does not express her likes and dislikes then anger and frustration can easily build up and the relationship will begin to disintegrate. She has not discovered that differences do not mean instant disapproval. She may find herself feeling close to one person, believing that they are everything to her, and then as differences are expressed or she feels let down in any way, she interprets it as rejection and runs. She will also go on repeating old patterns and creating situations where she manipulates protection from others.

**3. Emotional dependency.** This occurs when someone believes that the ongoing presence and nurturing of another person is necessary in order to feel secure. Emotional dependency is probably taking place when either person in the friendship:

- experiences frequent jealousy, possessiveness and a desire to have the person to themselves, viewing other people as a threat to the relationship
- wants to spend all the time alone with this friend and becomes frustrated when this doesn't happen
- becomes irrationally angry or depressed when the person withdraws slightly
- loses interest in other friendships
- becomes preoccupied with the friend's appearance, personality, problems and interest
- is unwilling to make short or long range plans that do not include the other person
- is unable to see the other's faults realistically
- refers frequently to the other in conversation or feels free to 'speak for' the other
- exhibits an intimacy and familiarity with this friend that causes others to feel uncomfortable in their presence[5]

Sufferers are often afraid that those who are close to them do not love them despite being told they are loved. They have experienced betrayal and so find it hard to trust. Recovery involves learning to trust. Trust does not 'just happen' it comes through the nurturing of others, the experience of the deep love of God, and the sufferer's willingness gradually to get close, knowing that her world will not fall apart even if friendships fail.

The turning-point in overcoming these patterns usually comes when the sufferer no longer relies on others as the source of her security, finds a meaningful relationship with God, and develops friendships with a variety of people.

## Fleeing perfectionism

'As long as we believe perfection offers an answer to our emptiness and pain, we will continue to pursue any route that promises we can achieve it'.[6] Whilst it is good to have high standards there is a level of perfectionism which is unhealthy – where, if things are not exactly as the person wants them, she is driven into the depths of despair or the slums of self-condemnation. There is a problem when people believe that perfectionism is necessary in order to have good self-esteem or to feel accepted by others.

Being a perfectionist does not always mean being neat and tidy. There are many people who are perfectionists in their thinking, believing that they *should* be perfect or they *ought* to do better. With perfectionists there is an inbuilt sense of guilt and they feel very sensitive to what other people think, finding it hard to feel accepted by God and others. Perfectionists tend to 'play it safe' and not take risks because not doing a job well results in unwanted anxiety.

As with so many things, healing is preceded by understanding how the problem developed. Perfectionism may have come out of high standards set in childhood; the sufferer's own need to please; growing up without having known privacy or an individual identity; not having been allowed to express herself in spontaneous, childish ways.

'Without flexibility, there is no freedom'.[7] Freedom comes in taking on board the truth that God's love is more valuable and more lasting than the approval of other people. Change must be gradually introduced. In her recovery Rebekah discovered that she had to *allow* herself to make mistakes. It was liberating for her to make a mistake and learn that there were still people around who did not think any less of her. The sufferer needs to accept that she, like everyone else, is someone with failures and weaknesses. She must choose not continually to make comparisons with what could have been, or with other people, and must begin to set realistic standards. She needs also to let go of the fantasy of a 'perfect family', of which she considers she has been deprived.

## Establishing self-assertiveness

The sufferer has grown up not knowing what she needs or wants and feeling much shame. Learning about healthy assertiveness can be a way of reclaiming what was lost. She may feel afraid of the consequences of being assertive or, if she is a Christian, assume that being assertive is wrong. Being assertive is not being aggressive, manipulative or hostile. It is realising that both her and other people's opinions and feelings count: '… equality is one of the most important hallmarks of assertive behaviour'.[8] Self-assertiveness comes out of self-acceptance and self-confidence.

Amongst other things, assertiveness means that she:

- takes responsibility for herself, her feelings, thoughts and behaviour
- respects herself, both as a person and in the things she does
- realises that she is not responsible for other adults' feelings and actions
- asks for time to think things over or for questions to be repeated, if needed
- recognises her own needs and wants separately from the needs and wants of others
- asks for what she wants instead of hoping that someone will guess

- expresses her feelings without feeling threatened
- allows herself to make mistakes and recognises that it's OK to do so
- allows herself to give and receive compliments
- recognises the need to be motivated by love not anger
- allows herself to be happy and to enjoy her successes
- admits she has the right to change her mind
- recognises her limits and is able to say 'No'
- accepts constructive criticism and rejects destructive criticism
- respects other people and their right to be assertive.

Learning to be assertive is a process. It is useful first for the sufferer to think through the situations in which she would like to develop this skill. As the sufferer attempts to put self-assertiveness into practice she needs to be aware of her body – it is not productive to express assertiveness in words and communicate a different message through body language. She must practice making eye-contact, standing up straight, speaking out, etc.

Two vital areas Natalie had to look at were stopping using food and weight to express how she felt and establishing healthy boundaries with others. For a long time she had used being underweight as a way of expressing 'No' to sexual advances – instead she had to learn how to verbalise the word 'No'. Natalie also had to set limits with her mother. Her mother was over-involved in Natalie's life, despite Natalie having lived away from home for seven years. Still loving her mother, she had to express her dislike of her mother's interference and that it was driving her away from the family.

## Discovering self-acceptance

Everything discussed in the recovery section of this book (the last seven chapters) is made more possible as the sufferer discovers self-acceptance. Self-acceptance is first the acknowledgement that strengths *and* weaknesses make for a balanced life. It involves the sufferer accepting herself despite negative feelings; choosing not to abandon herself when life becomes hard; respecting her values, opinions and ideas; accepting that she is both unique and equal to everyone else. Sometimes the person needs to speak out loud to herself the words 'I accept myself'. This is not arrogance. It comes out of the truth that the only reason any of us is acceptable is because of the price which Jesus paid for our sins when He died on the Cross.

The sufferer has been so used to putting herself down that she has focused on only the negative. Most people find it easier to speak of what they don't like about themselves than what they do like. When given the chance to look at the positive aspects a person can surprise herself as to how much there is of value in her life. I remember, years after having recovered from anorexia, joining in a group therapy session. The therapist asked us to write down ten things we liked about ourselves. I found I could list only five:

1. Being artistic
2. Feeling compassion for others
3. Having achieved
4. Being keen to learn from previous hurts and use them for good
5. Being gentle

As I read them out to the therapist she encouraged me to state five more. 'Recently several people have commented that I am intelligent', I said hesitantly, waiting for her to laugh.

'And are you?', she replied.

'Well, sort of'. I wanted to hide.

'Everything I've seen of you so far indicates to me that you are intelligent Helena'. I was touched by her remark but inside I was thinking of how I had messed up my

GCSE's through being ill with anorexia and failed one of the exams I took early – the one I most wanted. Then again I had done well at college, won a national award and come top in my counselling training. 'Own it Helena', the therapist urged, 'Say, "I am intelligent"'. I said the words out aloud: 'I am intelligent'. How good it felt. God had gifted me so who was I to hurl the gift back at Him? I was discovering new aspects of myself.

People with eating disorders do not seem to apply the same rules to themselves as they do to others. The sufferer needs to begin to ask herself, 'Would I react to a hurting friend in the same way as I react to myself when I am hurting?' Learning to treat and be kind to herself is part of the healing process. This is different for everyone. It may be a long soak in the bath, a massage, a visit to the theatre, a holiday, etc.

Accepting her body is not easy for someone suffering from an eating disorder but it is important. Throughout the sufferer's illness the body has been her main focus. Acceptance is made possible as she sees the physical as only *one* part of herself and lets go of having to attain the perfect image. It is easier to accept the physical as she puts it into perceptive with the rest of her as a person. Although the physical is not the most important aspect it must not be ignored. Making the most of herself, such as developing good dress sense, choosing a hairstyle which suits her, using make-up in a way which brings out the best in her, gives her confidence. Still, however much she concentrates on the physical, it is her qualities of character which remain the most valuable and commend her to others.

Many character qualities have their negative aspects, in addition to their positive aspects. When a person does not have much self-worth it is too easy to look only at the negative. I am a very sensitive person and at one stage I can remember thinking, as people's words wounded me deeply, that I was almost too sensitive to live. Gradually I began to look at what I liked about my sensitivity: it is my sensitivity which enables me to understand and feel for others. If we choose the helpful aspect of a quality we must also accept and learn how to cope with the unhelpful aspect. I am in the process of discovering, when hurt by others' comments, to look at whether I am over-reacting and in need of changing my outlook. Frequently I have to remind myself of the fact that it is my sensitivity which enables me to discern when someone else is struggling. This is something I would be sad to be without.

# 13 | PLAYING NEW MESSAGES

The Bible says: 'Be careful how you think; your life is shaped by your thoughts' (Proverbs 4:23 GNB). How the sufferer thinks affects the way she feels, the choices she makes and to what extent she pursues true life.

Many sufferers assume that the things which happen to them and around them are what cause their negative feelings. Thinking in this way results in a sense of helplessness because it means that if circumstances are not ideal the person could be in pain indefinitely. Some people puzzle over why a single remark can cause inner torment, feeling that their only option is to avoid contact with those who may say something to hurt them. Other people are unable to explain why they feel low.

Albert Ellis, a clinical psychologist, developed what he terms The ABC Theory of Emotion:[1]

    A = the activating event
    B = the belief system
    C = the consequent emotion

His point is that it is not the *event* in itself which results in the emotion, but rather what the person *believes* or *says* to herself about the event. This is why two people faced with the same circumstances can feel and act quite differently from each other.

Let's create an imaginary situation to illustrate this principle. A young woman is standing at a bus stop. The only person she really trusts walks by without even a 'Hello'. The young woman immediately experiences a stabbing pain. Several hours into the day she feels depressed. A few days later she is still low, and tends to push others away. Could an event such as someone just walking by cause intense pain? Yes! This grows out of what the young woman said to herself about her friend in the seconds following the event: 'She doesn't care for me any more'. The words she spoke to herself are perfectly understandable for someone who has been wounded in the past, but they are irrational. If, instead, she had said: 'Obviously my friend didn't see me; I'll phone her later and see if we can get together', the young woman's feelings would have been different. She might have been a little disappointed that she had been missed but not mortally wounded and forced to withdraw from people.

## Destructive messages

Some psychologists call the things we believe or say – about a situation, to ourselves or about other people – self-talk.

Much of the sufferer's self-talk stems from her childhood and painful life experiences. For example, a child whose parents only affirm her when she achieves well may grow up with the belief 'I must do everything perfectly in order to feel of worth'. Words spoken repeatedly by a child's parents, teachers, school friends, or her own interpretations, can influence quite dramatically the way a child views herself and her world:

- 'You never do anything right'
- 'I can't trust you'
- 'You're bad/wicked'
- 'What will the neighbours think?'
- 'You don't belong in our group'
- 'Fatty; sausage legs; moon-face; ugly features'
- 'You ought to have known better'
- 'You ought to do better'
- 'You're a hopeless case'

- 'Bad things only happen to bad people'
- 'People won't like you if you cry'

By frequently hearing negative things about herself a child will eventually begin to behave as though they are true. 'You don't belong in our group' she might translate into 'I'm not liked'. This can cause the child to withdraw from others, then others give up approaching her, which confirms that she's not liked. She begins to wonder why she's not liked: 'Maybe I'm not good enough'; 'Perhaps I'm different'. In time, she is telling herself: 'I'm a failure, different from other people and utterly bad'.

Through destructive and negative words the potential sufferer grows up with a distorted picture of herself. If someone hears the words stupid, ugly, hopeless, etc. used to describe her too often she will begin to see herself in this light. Her self-worth and self-confidence drop lower by the day. Like anything negative which is focused on too much, the distortion becomes greater. Distortions do not just disappear, they need the real truth to erase the lies. If, all my life, I have been told that I am bad I know no different: I am bad. I will only know different when someone defines good and bad and tells me that I am *not* bad. Even then it will take a long time to correct what I have been told for twenty-odd years.

Not changing her self-talk and the way she views herself will affect the way the sufferer relates to other people. Dag Hammerskjöld said: 'A man who is at war with himself will be at war with others'.[2]

*Troublesome self-talk*
It is helpful for the sufferer to make a list of the possible sentences she says to herself.

**About the eating disorder**
- 'I can't change'
- 'I'll never like my body'

- 'Being thin means everything will be OK'
- 'If I could just lose weight I'd feel different'
- 'I'll never stop putting on weight'
- 'I can't go out to a meal if I can't be sick afterwards'
- 'I have to take laxatives otherwise … '
- 'No one understands'

## About herself
- 'I must never be wrong'
- 'I should think only "proper" thoughts'
- 'What I want doesn't count'
- 'I'm stupid'
- 'I could and ought to do better'
- 'I should always be strong'
- 'I should never upset other people'
- 'If people really cared they would know what I need'
- 'People don't like me'
- 'To be accepted I have to be how others want me to be'
- 'When someone is angry with me it's my fault'
- 'If I don't do what people want then they won't like me'
- 'I must always make other people happy'

## Exaggerated thoughts
- 'People being angry or criticising me is *intolerable*'
- 'It's *disastrous* when things go wrong'
- 'If I'm angry it means I'm *horrible*'
- 'If I'm in pain it's *unbearable* not to have relief straight away
- 'Being fat's the *worst* thing in the world'

## Black and white thinking
- 'If I eat this biscuit I'll get fat'
- 'If I don't starve I'll never stop eating'
- 'If I don't get all A grades I'm a failure'
- 'If I'm not liked by everyone I must be hated by everyone'
- 'If I'm not good I'm bad'

It is said that we speak to ourselves at a rate of 1,300 words per minute.[3] If most of those words are self-condemnatory no wonder the sufferer walks around in a perpetual state of feeling as though she is stuck at the bottom of a pit full of thick mud with a suction beneath her feet.

## Behind feelings

As the sufferer finds herself experiencing pain it is worth her asking what she might have said to herself to trigger the emotion. She will also need to look at the sentences she regularly says to herself and discover if these have their roots in childhood, and find healing for the hurt in these words.

There are certain questions she can ask herself to help her to consider whether her thoughts are causing problems, such as:

- Am I thinking in all-or-nothing terms?
- Am I condemning myself as a total person on the basis of a single event?
- Am I concentrating on my weaknesses and forgetting my strengths?
- Am I blaming myself for something which is not my fault?
- Am I taking something personally which has little or nothing to do with me?
- Am I expecting myself to be perfect?
- Am I using a double standard – how would I view someone else in my situation?
- Am I paying attention only to the black side of things?
- Am I overestimating the chances of disaster?
- Am I exaggerating the importance of events?
- Am I fretting about the way things ought to be instead of accepting and dealing with them as they come?
- Am I assuming I can do nothing to change my situation?

- Am I predicting the future instead of experimenting with it?[4]

It is important for the sufferer to develop the habit of looking at all sides of a bad situation before deciding that it has something to do with her faults. Also, she should begin to ask herself what the evidence is when she declares that something is 'terrible'; 'unbearable'; 'disastrous'.

## Challenging thinking

As thoughts arise, or having asked herself what thoughts lie behind her negative feelings, the sufferer can begin to challenge these. Let's take examples from sentences used above:

**Thought** 'I must never be wrong'.

**Challenge** 'Is it possible to be right all the time?'

**Thought** 'I should never upset other people'.

**Challenge** 'Am I responsible for other people's feelings?'

**Thought** 'If people really cared they would know what I need'.

**Challenge** 'Is it fair to expect other people to guess what I need?'

There are four rules when challenging exaggerated or black and white thinking.[5]
1. If it's worth doing, it's worth doing even poorly.
2. Practice makes better, not perfect.
3. It's better to try and fail, than fail by not trying.
4. We should fail at half the things we try in life or we'll never know what we are accomplishing.

## Speaking truth

After a person has challenged her unhelpful thoughts she needs to work on correcting these.[6] In stopping to think about what she is saying to herself, and correcting the thought to one that is rational, positive and in line with biblical principles, what might have resulted in a low feeling can be turned into something constructive. Taking the examples we used for challenging the thoughts, let us replace the irrational thought with a rational one:

**Thought**  'I must never be wrong'.

**Truth**  'Being wrong is not comfortable, but just because I'm wrong doesn't mean other people are going to dismiss me'.

**Thought**  'I should never upset other people'.

**Truth**  'I can't avoid accidentally upsetting others sometimes and I am not responsible for their feelings or reactions'.

**Thought**  'If people really cared they would know what I need'.

**Truth**  'Just because a person doesn't guess what I need doesn't mean they don't care. It's unreasonable to expect them to guess, and it's up to me to ask'.

As the sufferer changes her thoughts so her feelings change. The more she practises asking herself what she is saying when in pain or depressed, the closer she will get to stopping her thoughts before they reach the stage of destructive feelings taking over. In time, some of her thinking will become intentionally realistic instead of automatically self-condemnatory.

Speaking truth to oneself can be very powerful. Truth about ourselves is based on the Truth, which is God's Word. We are:

- a chosen people (1 Peter 2:9 NIV)
- precious (Isaiah 43:4 TLB)
- loved (1 John 4:10 NIV)
- His sons and daughters (2 Corinthians 6:18 NIV)
- called (1 Thessalonians 5:24 NIV)
- an heir (Galatians 4:7 NIV)
- belonging to God (1 Peter 2:9 NIV)
- honoured (Isaiah 43:4 TLB)
- accepted (Romans 15:7 NIV)
- set free (Colossians 1:14 CEV)
- forgiven (Colossians 3:13 NIV)

Reminding herself of such words and speaking these to herself, instead of her usual derogatory words, will make a difference as to how the sufferer feels. The Book of Proverbs has wise sayings about the power of words: 'Thoughtless words can wound as deeply as any sword, but wisely spoken words can heal' (12:18 GNB); 'Kind words bring life, but cruel words crush your spirit' (15:4 GNB). Satan will use negative words to pull down and destroy the peace, joy, hope and self-respect of people, sucking them into the pit of misery and degradation.

Not only does God speak special words to the sufferer, He offers His help as she endeavours to make difficult changes in her life:

- 'I will not forget you! See, I have engraved you on the palms of my hands ... ' (Isaiah 49:15-16 NIV)
- 'If you are attacked and knocked down, you will know that there is someone who will lift you up again.' (Job 22:29 TLB)
- 'Do not be afraid – I will save you. I have called you by name – you are mine.' (Isaiah 43:1 GNB)

- 'But with everlasting kindness I will have compassion on you … ' (Isaiah 54:8 NIV)
- 'The mountains and hills may crumble, but my love for you will never end … ' (Isaiah 54:10 GNB)

What has to take place for the sufferer is a renewing of her mind. The Bible tells us: 'Do not conform any longer to the pattern of this world, but be transformed by the renewing of your mind.' (Romans 12:2 NIV) J. B. Phillips translates the same verse: 'Don't let the world around you squeeze you into its mould, but let God remake you so that your whole attitude of mind is changed … '

## Maintaining balance

Along the road of restoring her thinking each person will have her own experiences which she labels as 'terrible'. Most of these 'terrible' experiences will be unavoidable in life and so it can help to take a realistic look at them. One which is common for someone with an eating disorder is other people being angry with her. Below is an example of a realistic look at anger. The sufferer can create her own lists of other situations she experiences as 'terrible'.

1. Don't be upset every time someone becomes angry with you. It isn't a disaster. You *can* cope with it effectively.
2. Don't shape you behaviour just to prevent others' getting upset with you; they will anyway and when they do it's their problem not yours.
3. Be careful not to reward the angry outbursts of others. Ignore them when they yell at you, but be very attentive when they speak reasonably.
4. Don't be intimidated. Speak up and say: 'Please talk to me reasonably'.
5. Be kind and loving. Just because someone shows anger to you doesn't mean you have to be angry back. Say words such as: 'I am sorry you are feeling bad. Can

I do anything to help you feel less upset?'

6. When there is truth in an accusation directed at you, admit it. Don't lie and defend yourself. You don't have to be right all the time. Say words like: 'It's true Mum. I have been hiding food, it was wrong of me and I am sorry. But please can we talk about this calmly? In fact I would find it easier to talk first to someone from the self-help group and will do so'.

7. Give others the right to be angry with you sometimes and don't be shocked and offended when it happens. If you insist everyone sees and respects you as the 'perfect human being with no faults', you will be deeply disappointed ... Sometimes the anger vented at you by someone will have nothing to do with you. You may merely be the target for someone's frustrations and unhappiness. Learn to identify such things, refusing to take personally every word spewed at you.[7]

Changing her thinking, for the sufferer, should be in conjunction with, not as a replacement of, working through the pain, altering her behaviour patterns and pursuing true life. Otherwise the change will only be superficial.

Recovery is a process and so there are bound to be days when the sufferer goes backwards. It is easy at this stage for her to become disillusioned and assume that, statistically, she is part of the percentage which will remain ill for the rest of their lives. One of the most productive lessons a sufferer can learn is continually to use her pain and disappointment to motivate her towards healing. Falling down does not mean a person is defeated – it is the lack of picking herself up after having fallen which is a sign of defeat. The Bible also reminds us: 'If they fall it isn't fatal, for the Lord holds them with His hand'. (Psalm 37:24 TLB)

For the non-Christian, healing possibly ends with this chapter, although there are probably aspects of the next chapter which she can take on board. Her recovery is very much dependent on her own ability to keep going or on her circumstances. This doesn't mean to say that a non-Christian can't make a full recovery. It is just different from recovery for the Christian, who is called to rely no longer on her own strength, but on God and on a growing relationship with Jesus.

Sheena, who is a Christian in the process of recovery from anorexia, said:

> "Frequently now I cry out to God to re-order my thoughts, to bring truth, light and peace to the situation. He does, showing me the futility of what I am doing to myself – a vicious circle of depriving and satisfying, emptying and filling, and getting nowhere. Sometimes I still give in to the fear and the negative self-talk but I now see that I am choosing to do that, to be completely dictated to by old tapes playing in my head, to pursue a death course. I can choose life or death".

As we will see in the final chapter, Sheena goes on to discover a deeper level in her healing.

# 14 | PURSUING TRUE LIFE

Pursuing true life does not mean just changing behaviour, it means seeking growth and maturity. Growth must be cultivated, and in order to experience this the sufferer needs first to recognise what prevents growth. If she has not worked through her emotional problems and is still holding on to a distorted picture of herself and of God the result will be stunted growth. Another stumbling block is a loss of commitment to recovery. Growth is also restricted if communication is poor or lacks honesty and openness. 'We were created to live in relationship with others and relationships are maintained largely through communication'.[1]

Selwyn Hughes suggests ten marks of maturity:

1. A willingness to accept the responsibility for being what we are
2. Dependent trust
3. An obedient heart
4. A willingness to face and feel everything that goes on inside us
5. A deep personal joy
6. The ability to relate to others
7. A strong sense of morality
8. A healthy sense of self-worth
9. A continued thirsting after God
10. An overflowing love[2]

'Maturity is not the absence of struggle, but the ability to struggle well; it is not the absence of pain, but the ability to know God in the midst of pain'.[3]

Growth and maturity are working towards Jesus' words: 'Be perfect, therefore, as your heavenly Father is perfect' (Matthew 5:48 NIV). Most sufferers will interpret this as a command to be a perfectionist, failing in nothing. But the Greek word for perfection, teleios, is used not just in connection with goodness but with being 'complete', 'fully grown', 'mature', which, to me, signifies being 'made whole'.

The visible evidence of maturity is relating in love. As people learn to love, the internal structures that sustain their emotional and psychological ills are eroded'.[4]

## Fulfilment

Maturity becomes possible as people turn to God to meet their needs for love, nurturing, self-worth, security, acceptance and recognition. If God made us, there is a depth of need within us which only He can satisfy. Whilst people and circumstances can provide us with a strong sense of our needs being met, there is a problem when those close to us fail us, reject us, die, or circumstances change for the worse. God does not require us to ignore what can be found in other people or what we can give to other people, but He does require us to turn to Him as provider. For instance, our worth as people should be found in who we are in Christ and His love for us, not in what the media dictates, how successful we are, our marital status or what we look like. Our worth in Christ and His love for us cannot change, everything else can.

There is so much that the sufferer can learn in connection with her needs and God's provision. But first she must be aware of how deep her needs are in order to know the sufficiency of God meeting those needs. Let's look at a few truths.

**Love.** Initially the sufferer may find it difficult to accept the unconditional love of God because she is used to love with conditions. If she is still holding on to the belief that she is a bad person then she can easily feel that God does not love her. If a person blocks off her negative emotions she will also block off her positive ones to an extent. If this is the case she can struggle to *feel* God's love.

It is hard both to experience and give love if we do not love ourselves. In Matthew 19:19 we are told to love our neighbour as ourself. God desires us to love and care for ourselves, which is possible through His love for us. Other people demonstrate God's love, but the sufferer also needs to experience it personally. Experiencing comes through understanding the nature and the depth of God's love and spending time with Him. Sheena found a difference in her life when she discovered the depth of God's love. She wrote:

> "The most significant thing that has happened since I last saw you is that I have come to know Jesus' love for me in an intimate and personal way. In fact it's the most amazing thing to have happened in my whole life. One morning I was crying, and said to God: 'Something's missing'. Suddenly it was as if a fog lifted and I knew that Jesus Christ, the Son of God, had died for me. I could feel His love and I just wept with joy. It was the first time for many years that I felt joy, or any feeling other than despair for that matter. I knew that I still faced the same problems I'd faced ten minutes earlier, that nothing had changed, and yet at the same time, everything was completely different".

**Self-worth.** Sheena went on to realise that her worth is found in God because she is made in His image. 'God showed me that just as when I write a piece of music it is an expression of *me*, so when He made me I was an expression of *Him*. Even though I am a tiny creature, I am made in God's image'.

To feel of worth the sufferer must learn to be content

with herself; to look at what God has given her rather than what she lacks in comparison with others. To know, as it says in Psalm 139, that she is fearfully and wonderfully made. 'A healthy self-image is seeing yourself as God sees you – no more and no less'.[5] There is too much emphasis on outward appearances in order to feel of worth. Melvin Kinder, a psychiatrist, says: 'We have lost the truth that human beings should not be improved but should be nurtured'.[6]

**Acceptance.** The sufferer, like all of us, is owned by God and her life was paid for through the death of Jesus, who died that she might be acceptable in God's eyes. She does not have to achieve or prove anything, or conform to media or peer pressure in order to be accepted. She only has to *be*. Peter reminds us in his letter that we should not be unduly concerned with outward appearances but rather: 'Be beautiful inside, in your hearts, with the lasting charm of a gentle and quiet spirit which is so precious to God'. (1 Peter 3:4 TLB)

Sheena explained that, for her, the fact that she is owned by God also brought home the reality that she is not actually her own: 'I am the work of God's hands, and so I don't have the right to destroy myself'. If the sufferer chooses to believe that Jesus died for her and acknowledges Him as her Lord then she will also know eternal life. If not, the fact is that God still loves her.

## *Dependence*
One of the most important components of recovery is giving God the control:

> "Even though we pray about our challenges and problems, all too often what we really want is strength to accomplish what we've already decided is best for ourselves and others. Meanwhile we press on with our own priorities and plans. We remain the

scriptwriter, casting director, choreographer and producer of the drama of our own lives, in which we are the star performer".[7]

I remember with my own experience of anorexia giving God the control was the most feared aspect. I felt that if I gave Him the control then I would be in danger of losing self-control and would plunge head-first into the pits of self-indulgence. Then it dawned on me that the fruits of the Spirit are love, joy, peace, patience, kindness, goodness, faithfulness, humility and *self-control*. (Galatians 5:22-23) In handing over the control the sufferer is acknowledging that God is directing her life, instead of herself. This does not mean that she will be out of control or manipulated. Sheena discovered the purpose of her eating disorder and how it kept her from being dependent on God:

"My anorexia was a bid for self-dependence. It was my attempt to be in complete control of all that affected me; to run away from painful realities. It was the 'perfect' world where I made the rules, and I kept or broke them. Cramming my head with calorie-counting, weights and exercise plans was an effort to occupy every available brain cell with what I could control. I decided that X calories = safe and that X + 100 = unsafe; that I had to walk for one hour a day, that stillness was absolutely not safe. Things became habits and habits became compulsions. The 'perfect' world was really a nightmare of one rule after the next, and agony if, for some reason, my plans were thwarted. The most insidious thing about anorexia is that is seems to take on a life of its own. What starts out as a series of choices develops into a frightening master, cracking the whip at a driven slave".

Giving God the control is not a one-off thing. Every time

we realise that we have taken it back we surrender it to Him again (without self-condemnation). He is the One who is ultimately in control; we are the ones who take responsibility for what He gives us to do.

Before a sufferer is willing to allow God to be in control of her life she may have to change the way she sees God. Our mental picture of God is often based on significant people in our childhood. The sufferer may see God as:

- angry and ready to punish
- unable to please
- over-controlling
- distant, rigid and authoritarian
- someone who's too busy to listen
- unable to cope with her emotions
- more interested in her performance than her as a person

Knowing what God is really like means knowing the character of God. Some of His traits are:

- unfailing love (Psalm 36:7 NIV)
- faithful to His promises (Isaiah 30:18 TLB)
- truly good (Luke 18:10 TLB)
- has compassion (Psalm 145:9 NIV)
- slow to anger (Numbers 14:18 NIV)
- full of wisdom (Psalm 36:6 TLB)
- forgiving (1 John 1:9 NIV)
- rich in mercy (Ephesians 2:4 NIV)
- can do anything (Job 42:2 TLB)
- does not change (James 1:17 NIV)
- full of grace and truth (John 1:14 NIV)
- tender kindness (Psalm 89:1 TLB)
- perfect in His understanding (Job 36:5 TLB)
- just and fair (Deuteronomy 32:4 TLB)

Dependence on God, or seeing Him as Father, might be hard for some sufferers because they see this as once again being powerless. The important difference is that God does not impose Himself on us – He gives us *choice*. Jesus says: 'If you are tired from carrying heavy burdens, come to me and I will give you rest' (Matthew 11:28 CEV). He does not force us to come or punish us for not doing so. Instead He offers to exchange our load for His, which He says is light (Matthew 11:29–30). Whether or not we take Him up on the offer is entirely up to us.

What does God do for the sufferer if she cries out to Him?

- comforts us when we are in trouble (2 Corinthians 1:4 CEV)
- is a father to the fatherless (Psalm 68:5 TLB)
- a tower of safety (Psalm 18:2 TLB)
- gives strength and mighty power to His people (Psalm 68:35 TLB)
- gives families to the lonely (Psalm 68:6 TLB)
- will spread His wings over you and keep you secure (Psalm 91:4 CEV)
- is your protector, and He won't go to sleep or let you stumble (Psalm 121:3 CEV)
- will rescue you from your captivity (Deuteronomy 30:3 TLB)

## Repentance

I have said that honesty is essential to change. From honesty the sufferer needs to move to repentance and on to bold love:

> "Honesty removes the pleasant, antiseptic blandness of denial. Repentance strips away self-contempt and other-centred hatred and replaces it with humility, grief and tenderness. Bold love increases power and freedom through the exhilaration of loving as we are made to love ... Honesty and repentance are pre-conditions for life, but love sets the soul free to soar

through the damage of the past and the unrequited passion of the present ... forgiveness is the energy that propels the damaged man or woman toward the freedom to love".[8]

Repentance means turning around, but when the eating disorder sufferer considers repentance, of what should she be repentant? Not eating correctly? What the sufferer needs to repent of is the fact that she has tried to make her life work separately from God. The Bible declares: 'My people have committed two sins: They have forsaken me, the spring of living water, and have dug their own cisterns, broken cisterns that cannot hold water'. (Jeremiah 2:13 NIV) The sufferer may also need to repent of wounding other people in trying to protect herself.

Repentance results in Godly sorrow, which is different from just being sorry. Godly sorrow is being sorry in such a way that the person wants to change, not just feeling rotten about what she has done. This comes out of recognising how some of her choices have hurt God and others. It does not result in dwelling on faults; after Godly sorrow a person moves on to joy, she no longer stays with a feeling of 'Oh look what a terrible person I am'.

With God at the centre of her life the sufferer can leave behind unhealthy patterns such as self-pity or manipulation. Leaving behind old patterns is not easy and there is the fear of emptiness without them, but the promise of Jesus is that those who put their trust in Him will not be left without. Jesus said, "If you are thirsty, come to me and drink! Have faith in me, and you will have life-giving water flowing from deep inside you, just as the Scriptures say". Jesus was talking about the Holy Spirit, who would be given to everyone that had faith in Him'. (John 7:37-39 CEV)

*Forgiveness*
The sufferer cannot forgive until she acknowledges that

there is something hurtful in her past. A mistake which is often made within the Church is that forgiveness is asked of the sufferer too soon – she feels condemned for her unforgiving attitude and may withdraw from working towards recovery. True forgiveness cannot take place until she has worked through many things, including her feelings of powerlessness, betrayal, shame, self-hatred, anger, the child inside, and grief. God's forgiveness for any wrong she had done will be forthcoming, but there are two more aspects of forgiveness – forgiving those who have hurt her and forgiving herself.

Forgiveness of those who have hurt the sufferer does not mean instant, unlimited reconciliation. Whilst forgiveness usually leads to reconciliation there are some situations where this may be delayed or not possible. A situation where reconciliation is unable to take place may be where a father is still an active abuser and the married daughter he has abused has children – reconciliation may risk abuse of his grandchildren. 'Forgiveness is unrestrainable and unilateral. Nothing can ever stop us from forgiving anyone at any time. But the other person(s) can block unlimited reconciliation by denying the truth.[9]

The sufferer also needs to learn to forgive herself – for hurting herself, for abusing her body, or for failing to love. Forgiving herself means learning from mistakes instead of denying they exist or condemning herself for not being perfect. Forgiving oneself can often be harder than forgiving others or receiving God's forgiveness. I used to struggle with this terribly until one day I was faced with some strong truths by a colleague. 'If God has forgiven you, Helena', she said, 'then in not forgiving yourself you are saying that God's forgiveness is not good enough – you are placing your judgement higher than God's judgement'. I felt dumbstruck for a second and then intensely angry. How could she say such a thing! I couldn't stop thinking about it all evening and realised that the reason for this was because it was true. Since then, every time I have held onto self-condemnation I have reminded myself of those words.

If we do not forgive ourselves, it is also much harder to forgive others. 'The same executioner who screams: "Off with their heads!" every time we discover yet another way our parents abandoned us emotionally is the executioner who is out to get us every time we make a mistake'.[10] There is a point at which it becomes necessary to forgive in order to move on in life. As Dwight Lee Wolter says:

"When we hold onto rage at our parents, we are still holding onto our parents. When we let go of the rage, we let go of the grip we allow our parents to have on us. There has been, perhaps, enough suffering all around … For me, forgiving my parents began to make more sense when I realised that, ultimately, not forgiving them was like punishing them by holding my breath. Yes, they became concerned. But I was the one who turned blue and passed out".[11]

## Endurance

I would urge those who are struggling with overcoming an eating disorder to keep working towards *full* recovery. The Bible says: 'But he who perseveres and endures to the end will be saved …'. (Matthew 10:22 Amplified Bible):

"Endurance has two aspects: on the one side it means the commitment on our part not to give up, a determination to go all the way through; on the other side it has to do with God's enablement. What God calls us to do, He gives us the grace to accomplish … Sometimes you might feel it's impossible to go through to the end, to endure. And that may be right! But when we come to the end of what is possible for us, then we can see God do the impossible. Faith has not begun until we believe God for the impossible".[12]

> I waited patiently for the Lord's
>    help;
> then He listened to me and heard my
>    cry.
> He pulled me out of a dangerous pit,
>    out of the deadly quicksand.
> He set me safely on a rock
>    and made me secure.
> He taught me to sing a new song,
>    a song of praise to our God.
> Many who see this will take warning
>    and will put their trust in the Lord.
> (Psalm 40:1-3 GNB)

## Kainos Trust
### for eating disorders

### What is Kainos Trust?

*Kainos* is a Christian Charitable Trust that supports eating disorder sufferers and their families. It is a non medical organisation working to motivate and equip people to move towards, and maintain, full recovery. The focus of *Kainos* is prayer, teaching and personal support. *Kainos* works with the whole person: physical, emotional and spiritual, and adheres to practical and biblical principles.

### What does Kainos mean?

The word *Kainos* is taken from New Testament Greek, meaning new. It indicates something that is qualitatively new. We believe that people who completely overcome an eating disorder have a qualitatively new life: it is not the old life restored, but one that has changed as a result of what they have learned through their experiences. The word Trust is also significant. It was chosen not only because *Kainos* is a Charitable Trust, but because trust is important in the context of helping people with eating disorders.

### How did Kainos Trust start?

*Kainos* was established in 1995 by Helena Wilkinson. Helena nearly died from anorexia as a teenager. However, whilst she was in hospital at the age of 16, a Christian lady who was on the same ward had a prophetic word for Helena: that she would come through the anorexia knowing Jesus, that her name would be in print and that she would be well known for having overcome anorexia. When Helena was 18 years old she became a committed Christian and subsequently overcame anorexia. During this time she wrote an autobiographical book *Puppet on a String*. As a result she was inundated with desperate cries for help from people with eating disorders.

Helena went on to train in counselling, write other books on various subjects and lecture internationally on eating disorders. Around ten years later she founded *Kainos Trust*, which became a Registered Charity in September 1996. *Kainos Trust* now has its own Administration & Teaching Centre in Gloucestershire.

### How do I benefit from Kainos Trust?

If you would like to take advantage of what *Kainos* has to offer you will need to register with *Kainos*. The reason we like you to register with us is that you will receive our quarterly newsletter *Kainos News* and gain an understanding of our approach to eating disorders. It is also important to us to work in the context of a relationship with you. You can then make use of what *Kainos* offers.

### What does Kainos offer?

**Teaching Days:** addressing relevant issues to sufferers, and those who care for them. In addition *Kainos* runs day seminars on *Understanding Eating Disorders* in both the UK and overseas.

**Open Days:** where you can meet the Team informally and learn more about the work of *Kainos* and hear testimonies of recovery.

**Drop-in Days:** where you can drop in to *The Lower George House* (The Kainos Administration & Teaching Centre) for encouragement, support and advice or the chance to meet new people.

**A Resource List:** offering a variety of tapes, books and booklets relevant to eating disorders. Some of the material is only available through *Kainos*.

**Prayer & Intercession:** giving people with eating disorders who join the opportunity to be prayed for every day by a devoted group of Christians who believe that prayer does make a difference.

**Support through Letters:** offering understanding, care and advice to both eating disorder sufferers and parents or spouses.

**Counselling Appointments:** addressing the physical, emotional and spiritual aspects of the eating disorder. Parents also have the opportunity to attend appointments for advice.

**Residential Courses:** offering a homely and caring environment in which to learn principles for overcoming an eating disorder. The courses which are teaching based are kept small to ensure as much individual care as possible. The aim is both to equip and motivate people to work through recovery at home.

To be included on the mailing list or for further enquiries please write, enclosing a Stamped Addressed Envelope:

Kainos Trust
The Lower George House
High Street
Newnham-on-Severn
Gloucestershire
GL14 1BS
Tel: 01594 516284 (admin queries only)
Fax: 01594 516704
Website: www.kainostrust.co.uk
E-mail: enquiries@kainos.freeserve.co.uk

# REFERENCES

## CHAPTER 1

1. J. B. W. Williams (ed.), *Diagnostic and Statistical Manual of Mental Disorders*, Third Edition Revised (American Psychiatric Association, Washington, DC 1987).
2. *Ibid.*
3. M. Lawrence and M. Dana, *Fighting Food*, (Penguin, London, 1990), p. 44.
4. M. Duker and R. Slade, *Anorexia Nervosa and Bulimia: How to Help* (Open University Press, Milton Keynes, 1988), p. 25.
5. J. Yager, H. E. Gwirtsman and C. K. Edelstein (eds.), *Special Problems in Managing Eating Disorders* (American Psychiatric Press, Washington, DC, 1992).
6. M. Lawrence (ed.), *Fed Up and Hungry* (The Women's Press, London, 1987), p. 229.

## CHAPTER 2

1. J. Bradshaw, *Healing the Shame that Binds You* (Health Communications, Deerfield Beach, Florida, 1988).
2. *Ibid.*
3. *Ibid.*, pp. 11-12.
4. P. Lambley, *How to Survive Anorexia* (Frederick Muller, London, 1983), p. 125.
5. H. Bruch, *The Golden Cage* (Open Books, London, 1978), p. 48.
6. M. Lawrence (ed.), *Fed Up and Hungry*, pp. 83-84.
7. M. Lawrence, *The Anorexic Experience* (The Women's Press, London, 1984), p. 51.
8. P. Lambley, *How to Survive Anorexia*, p. 188.
9. J. Welbourne and J. Purgold, *The Eating Sickness*,

*Anorexia, Bulimia and the Myth of Suicide by Slimming* (Harvester Press, 1984), p. 119.
10. *Ibid.*, p. 120.
11. M. Lawrence and M. Dana, *Fighting Food*.
12. M. Duker and R. Slade, *Anorexia Nervosa and Bulimia: How to Help*.

**CHAPTER 3**
1. M. Dana and M. Lawrence, *Women's Secret Disorder* (Grafton, London, 1988).
2. *Ibid.*, p. 42.
3. *Ibid.*
4. *Ibid.*, p. 54.
5. *Ibid.*, pp. 59-60.
6. *Ibid.*
7. M. Lawrence and M. Dana, *Fighting Food*, p. 48.

**CHAPTER 4**
1. S. Billigmeier, *Inner Eating* (Oliver Nelson, Nashville, Tennessee, 1991), p. XV111.
2. *Ibid.*
3. Dr J. Hollis, *Fat is a Family Affair* (Hazelden Educational Materials, Center City, Minnesota, 1985), p. 33.
4. H. Bruch in P. Maisner and J. Pulling, *Feasting and Fasting* (Fontana, London, 1985).
5. Dr F. Minirth, Dr P. Meier, Dr R. Hemfelt and Dr S. Sneed, *Love Hunger* (Highland, Guildford, 1991), p. 24.
6. P. M. Smith, *The Food Trap* (Creation House, Lake Mary, Florida, 1990), p. 27.
7. Minirth, Meier, Hemfelt and Sneed, *Love Hunger*.
8. M. Lawrence (ed.), *Fed Up and Hungry*.
9. M. Lawrence and M. Dana, *Fighting Food*, p. 62.
10. S. Orbach, *Fat is a Feminist Issue* (Arrow, London, 1986), p. 68.
11. *Ibid.*, p. 85.
12. *bid.*, p. 73.

**CHAPTER 5**

1. D. Carder, E. Henslin, J. Townsend, H. Cloud and A. Brawand, *Secrets of Your Family Tree* (Moody Press, Chicago, Illinois, 1991).
2. H. Bruch, *The Golden Cage*, p. 26.
3. P. Lambley, *How to Survive Anorexia*.
4. B. M. Dolan, et al., 'Family Features Associated with Normal Body Weight Bulimia', *International Journal of Eating Disorders*, vol. 9, no. 6 (1990).
5. P. Lambley, *How to Survive Anorexia*.
6. H. Bruch, *The Golden Cage*.
7. M. West, *Shame-Based Family Systems* (CompCare Pulishers, Minneapolis, Minnesota, 1982).
8. J. VanVonderen, *Tired of Trying to Measure Up* (Bethany House, Minneapolis, Minnesota, 1989).
9. M. Lawrence and M. Dana, *Fighting Food*.
10. Dr R. Hemfelt and P. Warren, *Kids Who Carry Our Pain* (Word Books, Milton Keynes, 1991), p. 60.
11. D. W. Winnicott, 'The Theory of the Parent-Infant Relationship' in *The Maturational Processes and the Facilitating Environment* (Hogarth Press, London, 1965).
12. M. Lawrence, *The Anorexic Experience*, p. 65.
13. P. Lambley, *How to Survive Anorexia*, p. 162.
14. M. Lawrence, *The Anorexic Experience*.
15. S. Minuchin, B. L. Rosman and L. Baker, *Psychosomatic Families: Anorexia Nervosa in Context* (Harvard University Press, Cambridge, Mass., 1978). [Own simplified words.]
16. J. Moorey, *Living with Anorexia and Bulimia* (Manchester University Press, 1991).
17. M. Lawrence (ed.), *Fed Up and Hungry*.
18. H. Bruch, *Eating Disorders: Obesity, Anorexia Nervosa and the Person Within* (Routledge and Kegan Paul, London, 1974).
19. P. M. Smith, *The Food Trap*, pp. 126; 128.
20. J. VanVonderen, *Tired of Trying to Measure Up*.

**CHAPTER 6**
1. Dr J. H. Lacey, 'A Bulimic Syndrome', at the Sixth World Congress of the International College of Psychosomatic Medicine (Montreal, October 1981).
1. S. Orbach, *Fat is a Feminist Issue*.
3. *Ibid.*, p. 94.
4. M. Woodman, *The Owl was a Baker's Daughter* (Inner City Books, Toronto, 1980).
5. Dr D. B. Allender, *The Wounded Heart* (CWR, Farnham, 1991).
6. A. G. Cole, 'Body and Soul: Eating Disorders as a Re-enactment of Sexual Abuse', paper delivered at the Sexual Abuse Lecture and Workshop Series (The Horsham Clinic, Amber, Pennsylvania, November 1992), p. 12.
7. C. StarDancer (ed.), 'Recovery Issues: Eating Disorders', *Survivorship*, vol. 2, no. 2 (February 1990), p. 4. [Name invented.]
8. A. G. Cole, 'Body and Soul: Eating Disorders as a Re-enactment of Sexual Abuse', p. 11.

**CHAPTER 7**
1. M. Lawrence and M. Dana, *Fighting Food*.
2. *Ibid.*, p. 14.
3. *Ibid.*, p. 14.
4. C. Wills-Brandon, *Learning to Say No* (Health Communications, Deerfield Beach, Florida, 1990), p. 73.
5. G. Roth, *Feeding the Hungry Heart* (Grafton, London, 1986).
6. K. Keating, *The Hug Therapy Book* (CompCare Publishers, Minneapolis, Minnesota, 1983).
7. K. Keating, *Hug Therapy 2* (CompCare Publishers, Minneapolis, Minnesota, 1987).
8. Dr J. Sturt, 'Low Self-Esteem – Untangling the Roots', *Carer and Counsellor*, vol. 3, no. 2 (Spring 1993), p. 39.
9. *Ibid.*, p. 37.

10. *Ibid.*
11. A. Beck, et al., *Cognitive Therapy of Depression* (Guildford Press, New York, 1979).
12. Dr J. Sturt, 'Low Self-Esteem – Untangling the Roots'.
13. M. Lawrence and M. Dana, *Fighting Food*.
14. R. S. McGee, *The Search for Significance* (Word Books, Milton Keynes, 1990).

*CHAPTER 8*

1. Yager, Gwirtsman and Edelstein, *Special Problems in Managing Eating Disorders*.
2. *Ibid.*
3. F. Cremona (ed.), 'Recovery', *ABNA Newsletter*, June/July 1992, p. 6.
4. G. Roth, *Breaking Free from Compulsive Eating* (Grafton, London, 1986), p. 176.
5. Ibid., p. 189.
6. J. Welbourne and J. Purgold, *The Eating Sickness, Anorexia, Bulimia and the Myth of Suicide by Slimming*, p. 55.
7. J. Hollis, *Humility vs Humiliation* (Hazelden Educational Materials, Center City, Minnesota, 1986), p. 16.
8. J. Hollis, *Fat is a Family Affair*, p. 9.
9. P. Lambley, *How to Survive Anorexia*.
10. M. Duker and R. Slade, *Anorexia Nervosa and Bulimia: How to Help*, p. 208.

*CHAPTER 9*

1. R. Slade, *The Anorexia Nervosa Reference Book* (Harper and Row, London, 1984), p. 77.
2. Winterbourne Therapeutic Community.
3. Cullen Centre, Edinburgh, Scotland.
4. Dr C. Freeman, 'Day Patient Treatment for Anorexia Nervosa', *British Review of Bulimia and Anorexia Nervosa*, vol. 6, no. 1 (1992).
5. Taken from a paper for patients at Winterbourne Therapeutic Community. [Name invented.]

6.  C. F. Hall, 'Art Therapy in the Treatment of Eating Disorders', (Dissertation for Art Therapy Diploma, Goldsworth College, University of London, 1986).
7.  M. Levens, 'Art Therapy with Eating Disordered Patients', *Inscape*, Summer 1987, p. 3.
8.  J. Murphy, 'The Use of Art Therapy in the Treatment of Anorexia Nervosa' in *Art as Therapy*, T. Daily (ed.) (Tavistock, London, 1984).
9.  M. Levens, 'Art Therapy with Eating Disordered Patients'.
10. J. Murphy, 'The Use of Art Therapy in the Treatment of Anorexia Nervosa'.
11. *Ibid.*, p. 101.

CHAPTER 10
1.  H. Pope, J. Hudson and J. Jonas, 'Bulimia Treated with Imipramine: a Placebo Controlled, Double Blind Study', *American Journal of Psychiatry*, vol. 140 (1983).
2.  R. E. Vath, *Counseling Those with Eating Disorders* (Word Publishing, Dallas, 1986).
3.  G. Roth, *Breaking Free from Compulsive Eating*, p. 30.
4.  F. Heckel, *Les Grandes et Petits Obesites* (Maison et Cie, Paris, 1911).
5.  B. French, *Coping with Bulimia* (Thorsons, Wellingborough, 1987), pp. 92-93.
6.  For more information see Leonard Mervyn, *Thorsons Complete Guide to Vitamins and Minerals* (Thorsons, Wellingborough, 1986).
7.  C. Lewis, *Common Questions about Nutrition* (unpublished), pp. 19-20.
8.  *Ibid.*, pp. 9-10.
9.  Dr S. Davis and Dr A. Stewart, *Nutritional Medicine* (Pan, London, 1987).

CHAPTER 11
1.  A. Dixon, *A Woman in Your Own Right* (Quartet, London, 1982).

2.  G. Roth, *Breaking Free from Compulsive Eating*, p. 226.
3.  E. Bass and L. Davis, *The Courage to Heal* (Cedar, London, 1990), p. 193.
4.  C. Lang, 'Discovering, Re-creating and Healing the Self Through Art and Dreams: Help for Persons with Eating Disorders', in *Controlling Eating Disorders with Facts, Advice and Resources*, R. Lemberg (ed.) (Oryx Press, Phoenix, 1992).
5.  Joanne Smith Bloom and Judy Biggs, *How to Say Goodbye, Working Through Personal Grief* (Aglow Publications, Lynnwood, Washington, 1990), p. 71. Copyright 1990. Used with permission.
6.  For more information on these concepts see Penny Parks, *Rescuing the 'Inner Child'* (Souvenir Press, London, 1990).
7.  A. Dickson, *A Woman in Your Own Right*.
8.  For more information on these concepts see H. Norman Wright, *Overcoming Your Hidden Fears* (Scripture Press, Amersham-on-the-Hill, 1990).
9.  P. Vredevelt, Dr D. Newman, H. Beverly and Dr F. Minirth, *The Thin Disguise* (Thomas Nelson, Nashville, 1992), pp. 168-169. (Adapted from Vredevelt & Rodriguez).
10. For more information on these concepts see Penny Parks, *Rescuing the 'Inner Child'*.

*CHAPTER 12*
1.  V. Frankl, in *Every Day with Jesus*, January/February 1993.
2.  M. Lawrence (ed.), *Fed Up and Hungry*, p. 101.
3.  Dr R. Hemfelt, Dr F. Minirth and Dr E. Meier, *Love is a Choice* (Thomas Nelson, Nashville, 1989).
4.  M. Lawrence and M. Dana, *Fighting Food*.
5.  L. Thorkelson Rentzel, *Emotional Dependency* (InterVarsity Press, Downers Grove, Illinois, 1984).
6.  M. A. Mayo, *Skin Deep* (Servant Publications, Ann Arbor, Michigan, 1992), p. 17.

7. J. Bradshaw, *Healing the Shame that Binds You*, p. 200.
8. A. Dickson, A *Woman In Your Own Right*, p. 13.

**CHAPTER 13**
9. Dr A. Ellis, *Reason and Emotion in Psychotherapy* (Citadel Press, Secaucus, New Jersey, 1964).
10. W. Backus and M. Chapian, *Telling Yourself the Truth* (Bethany House, Minneapolis, 1980), p. 35.
11. Don Dulaney, a social scientist from the U.S.A.
12. Beck and Emery in J. Moorey, *Living with Anorexia and Bulimia*, p. 112.
13. R. E. Vath, *Counseling Those with Eating Disorders*, p. 92.
14. For more information on these concepts see William Backus and Marie Chapian, *Telling Yourself the Truth*.
15. *Ibid.*, p. 60. [Example in no. 6 my own.]

**CHAPTER 14**
1. M. Pytches, 'A Journey to Maturity', *The Christian Counsellor*, vol. 2, no. 3 (Summer 1992), p. 9.
2. S. Hughes, *Every Day with Jesus*, January/February 1993.
3. Helena Wilkinson interviewing Tom Varney in *The Christian Counsellor*, vol. 2, no. 3 (Summer 1992), p. 13.
4. L. Crabb, *Understanding People* (Marshall Pickering, London, 1988), p. 199.
5. J. McDowell, *His Image My Image* (Scripture Press, Amersham-on-the-Hill, 1985), p. 34.
6. M. Kinder, *Going Nowhere Fast* (Prentice Hall Press, New York, 1990), p. 32.
7. L. Ogilvie, *12 Steps to Living Without Fear* (Word Books, Waco, Texas, 1987), p. 133.
8. Dr D. B. Allender, *The Wounded Heart*, pp. 181; 219.
9. S. D. Wilson, *Released from Shame* (InterVarsity Press, Downers Grove, Illinois, 1990), p. 170.
10. D. L. Wolter, *Forgiving Our Parents* (CompCare Publishers, Minneapolis, 1989).
11. *Ibid.*, pp. 47-48; 53.

12. F. McClung, *The Father Heart of God* (Kingsway, Eastbourne, 1985), pp. 98–99.

Further copies of this book

can be purchased from

www.kainostrust.co.uk

or

www.theway.co.uk.


If you are a bookseller and would like to sell this
book to your customers,
please contact

Harvest Fields Distribution
Unit 17 Churchill Business Park
Churchill Road
DONCASTER
DN1 2TF
UK

Tel: +44 (0)1302 367868
Fax: +44 (0)1302 361006